Transition to Success

Transition to Success

The Transition to University Program

Melinda S. Harper, PhD
Christine L. Allegretti, PhD

MOMENTUM PRESS HEALTH

Transition to Success: The Transition to University Program
Copyright © Momentum Press®, LLC, 2018.

First published in 2018 by
Momentum Press®, LLC
222 East 46th Street, New York, NY 10017
www.momentumpress.net

ISBN-13: 978-1-94664-608-8 (paperback)
ISBN-13: 978-1-94664-609-5 (e-book)

Momentum Press Psychology Collection

DOI: 10.5643/9781946646095

Cover and interior design by S4Carlisle Publishing Services Private Ltd., Chennai, India

First edition: 2018

10 9 8 7 6 5 4 3 2 1

Printed in the United States of America

Abstract

The transition to university life challenges many first-year students who experience the normative issues of adjustment during this pivotal year. A program designed to assist first-year students with this transition, the Transition to University (T2U) program, uses peer-led groups to provide support and information first-year students need to be academically and socially successful. This book is a manual for the T2U program that outlines weekly meetings for first-year students throughout their first year of university life. These weekly meetings are coled by advanced-level undergraduate students who facilitate discussion and offer support, advice, and strategies to be successful throughout the first year. The book also includes a description of a supervision practicum for the student leaders with assignments and suggested readings. Finally, the book includes suggestions for assessing the effectiveness of the program. This book is meant to be used in conjunction with the student leadership book *Transition to Success: Training Students to Lead Peer Groups in Higher Education* (Harper and Allegretti 2018).

Keywords

college student adjustment, first-year student adjustment, group dynamics, leadership training, peer mentors, student leaders, transition to university

Contents

Preface

The transition to university is a challenging yet exciting time in a first-year student's life. Many institutions of higher learning recognize this pivotal experience and target academic and social learning opportunities to assist first-year students with this transition. What may be most impactful on the adjustment to university life is how socially integrated first-year students feel with their peers and campus community. We know that deep and meaningful connections with peers are associated with positive adjustment. If students do not feel socially connected to the institution, they may not fully appreciate or take advantage of the academic and intellectual parts of campus life. Moreover, when they experience normative problems related to adjusting to their new life, they may not have the resiliency, support, or knowledge to cope successfully.

Connecting with other first-year students helps normalize issues and provides support during the transition. In addition, connecting with older and more experienced students offers the benefits of having mentors and positive role models. A programmatic approach to building campus connections can provide first-year students with the immediate advantage of a small peer group as they begin their college journey. In this book, we describe a guide for implementing a student leadership program for supporting first-year students in a group setting. The program provides an immediate "home base" for first-year students to connect with each other and with their experienced leaders. Through their shared experiences, these emerging adults may meaningfully delve into the complex issues commonly experienced by first-year students. Meeting regularly offers a consistent and dependable set of friends and peers who can offer social support, informative insight, and experience in identifying solutions to normative problems. The student leaders, in turn, benefit from the leadership experience by facilitating discussion of these issues, reflecting upon their past experiences, and learning how to create a sense of cohesion and community.

We introduced the Transition to University (T2U) program on our campus for several reasons. We hoped the program would facilitate the adjustment to university life, provide social support, and build a sense of connection and community for first-year students. A number of outcomes indicate the success of this program including positive social adjustment, increased sense of connection with the university, and higher retention to the third semester for first-year students who participated in the program. Since its inception in 2006, the T2U program remains a popular campus experience for first-year students as well as a valued leadership experience for advanced undergraduate students. This program provides an opportunity for student leadership, peer mentorship, and peer support through the transition to university life.

The Scope of This Book

In this book, we focus on the Transition to University (T2U) program and how institutions of higher education can implement this student leadership program to support first-year students in their transition to university life. We emphasize using advanced-level undergraduate students as leaders, supporters, and mentors to assist their first-year student peers throughout this normative, yet challenging, developmental experience. Specifically, the use of students as leaders within a group context provides first-year students with an immediate and available social community and peer support group.

This book is a manual for implementing a student leadership program targeting first-year students and their adjustment to university life. In Chapter 1, we present an introduction, history, empirical data, and a detailed description of the T2U program. Chapter 2 describes the supervision and training of the student leaders. Chapters 3 and 4 outline the fall and spring sessions of the T2U program. Finally, Chapter 5 details the assessment of the T2U program and first-year student adjustment. This book is meant to be read in conjunction with *Transition to Success: Training Students to Lead Peer Groups in Higher Education* (Harper and Allegretti 2018).

Acknowledgments

Many thanks to the people who were instrumental in establishing the T2U program at Queens University of Charlotte. First and foremost, we acknowledge Dr. S. Mark Pancer, who first introduced the T2U program to us in 2006. He graciously shared his knowledge and expertise with us, and we are grateful for his unconditional support and encouragement of our work. We especially want to thank his exceptional team of colleagues who also generously shared their time and advice as well: Susan Alisat, Dr. Mike Pratt, Dr. Thanh-Thanh Tieu, and Dr. Maxine Wintre.

Thanks also to our T2U student leaders whom we have been privileged to train and collaborate with since the beginning of the program. The program's success is a testament to their hard work, dedication, and commitment to their student peers and the university. We also extend our gratitude to our colleagues in the Department of Psychology, Student Life, Health and Wellness, and Academic Affairs at Queens University of Charlotte.

Thanks also to our reviewers, colleagues, and friends. We especially wish to thank Dr. Dorothy Roberts, Melissa Bodford, Dr. Rick Deitchman, Scott Fouts, and Allan Shub. We also extend our thanks to the staff at Momentum Press for their guidance toward the completion of this book.

Finally, we thank our spouses and families. This book would not have been possible without them.

CHAPTER 1

Introduction to the T2U Program

Transitioning from high school to college is an opportunity for growing intellectually and personally, creating new social connections, and establishing a sense of community within a new environment. This transition is not easy. During their first year of college, students are particularly susceptible to both psychological and physical symptoms of stress (Baker and Siryk 1984; Compas et al. 1986; Gall, Evans, and Bellerose 2000). Many experience loneliness (Cutrona 1982), depression (Fisher and Hood 1988; Wolf, Scurria, and Webster 1998), and homesickness (Scopelliti and Tiberio 2010; Thurber and Walton 2012) in addition to significant health concerns and problematic use of substances (Aspinwall and Taylor 1992; Sadava and Pak 1993; Wechsler et al. 2002). Not surprisingly, many of these students withdraw from the university within their first year (Hamilton and Hamilton 2006; Levitz and Noel 1989).

Both emotional and social factors are key influences on first-year students' adjustment to their new university life (Brooks and DuBois 1995; Gerdes and Mallinckrodt 1994; Pritchard and Wilson 2003; Rickinson and Rutherford 1995). For many of these students, the degree to which they "fit in" and perceive their university as a match for them has been associated with a number of outcomes, including student retention and positive social and academic adjustment (Wintre et al. 2008). Since the support of peers is an essential factor for first-year student adjustment (Brooks and DuBois 1995; Compas et al. 1986; Cutrona 1982; Gall et al. 2000; Tao et al. 2000), many institutions of higher learning have implemented a variety of programs to assist their new students. These include orientation programs, first-year experience seminars, and other formally organized small group activities (Barefoot 2005; Harper and Allegretti 2018; Oppenheimer 1984; Upcraft, Gardner, and Barefoot 2005).

One program, Transition to University (T2U), emphasizes the social aspect of first-year student adjustment (Ayers et al. 2006; Pancer, Pratt, and Alisat 2006; Pratt et al. 2000). This social support intervention has been associated with a variety of positive adjustment and outcome measures, including better overall adjustment, significantly higher social support, and significantly lower depression compared with first-year students who did not participate in the intervention (Ayers et al. 2006; Pratt et al. 2000). Mattanah and colleagues (2010) found that first-year students who participated in T2U in their fall semester reported lower levels of loneliness and higher levels of social support in the spring semester. Moreover, these first-year students reported a higher GPA in the first semester of their sophomore year compared with those who did not participate in T2U. Pancer et al. (2004) found that students who participated in T2U continued to score higher on measures assessing social support, adjustment, and self-esteem and lower on measures of perceived stress in their 4th year of study compared with students who did not participate in the program. Students from this sample who participated in the T2U program were also more likely to complete their degree, with only 7.8 percent leaving the university without completing their degree compared with 28 percent of students who did not participate in the T2U program.

In 2006, Queens University of Charlotte implemented the T2U program (Harper and Allegretti 2009a, 2013, 2015, 2018). This program was based on a template of the original program, *Bridge over Troubled Water: Easing the Transition to University* (Hunsberger et al. 2003). Since its inception at Queens, the T2U program has thrived at this institution and remains an active and popular program for first-year students. Key factors that contribute to its success are the characteristics of the university, the use of undergraduate students as peer leaders of the small discussion groups, and the training of these leaders. First, Queens is a small, liberal arts-based institution with an incoming first-year student class of approximately 400 students. Queens' small size and emphasis on the liberal arts allow first-year students from a variety of backgrounds and with a range of interests to find commonality and inclusion in the classroom and on campus. In addition, using junior- and senior-level undergraduate students as peer mentors and leaders of the small T2U groups enhances the connection and relationship between first-year students and their slightly older and more seasoned and experienced peers. Finally, the design of the training curriculum for student leaders as part of a practicum course in group dynamics and leadership further enhances the quality of the experience by ensuring student leaders receive ongoing training throughout the program (Harper and Allegretti 2015, 2018).

Implementing the T2U Program

Institutions of higher learning can implement the T2U program using minimal resources. The essential elements of the program are motivated and capable student leaders, faculty or staff program directors who are able to train and supervise the student leaders, and the space to conduct the T2U group sessions (Harper and Allegretti 2018). In addition, the manual provided in this book thoroughly outlines each weekly session and serves as a guide to student leaders and their training supervisors throughout the academic year. Institutions may vary on how many T2U groups to offer their first-year students. Since each T2U group requires two student leaders, program directors must have adequate time to supervise all leaders.

Description of the T2U Program

The T2U program uses a group format to foster social integration, a sense of belonging and inclusion, and the normalization of common situations and problems other young adults may experience. In addition, the session format encourages students to work proactively together to generate solutions to normative challenges and dilemmas that first-year students experience. Moreover, the program offers upper-class students the opportunity to develop and practice leadership skills and learn group dynamics through an applied experience (Harper and Allegretti 2015, 2018).

Beginning the T2U sessions as early in the semester as possible is essential. We recommend beginning the program within the first 2 weeks of classes. These 2 weeks are critical in the transition process since many first-year students no longer have the structure of orientation or other prescribed programs to assist them with organizing their time. Instead, first-year students now have the independence and flexibility to choose how to spend their time outside of classes. A priority for many students is socializing with their new peers and taking the first steps toward developing these new connections into meaningful friendships and relationships. For some students, these experiences during the first few days and early weeks of the first year of college can be overwhelming. Offering an immediately available place of support and a peer network may be instrumental in buffering normative stress experienced early on in the transition process.

Once the program begins, each T2U group meets once a week in small discussion rooms on campus. These groups meet in the evening for approximately 60 to 90 minutes. Each T2U group is comprised of approximately 8 to 10 first-year students and is facilitated by junior and senior students who serve as coleaders and mentors. During the weekly meetings, the coleaders encourage the first-year student group members to discuss their new life on campus and work together with their peers to identify and develop strategies that they can use to facilitate their adjustment.

Outline of the T2U Program

In the fall, groups meet at least 10 times throughout the semester to discuss topics relevant to their new life at the university. The schedule of session topics corresponds with typical events and experiences that occur during the fall semester of the first year of college. Following the first introductory meeting, the topic for the second session is developing new friendships and using campus resources. By the third session, many first-year students are likely developing their daily routines and can benefit from a discussion on how to balance their new academic and social lives. The fourth session provides first-year students with an opportunity to discuss more in depth their developing or current relationships. During the fifth session, student leaders encourage first-year students to discuss recent experiences related to challenging, or affirming, their personal values and beliefs. Following fall break, the sixth session provides first-year students with an opportunity to reconnect with each other and also reflect on their social support network both at home and on campus. The seventh session is at a point in the fall semester when students are considering their plans for the spring. This session serves as an opportunity for student leaders to assist first-year students with their registration for spring classes and plans for the upcoming semester. As first-year students begin to prepare for final projects and upcoming exams, the eighth session serves as a reminder of the importance of healthy habits and balanced maintenance of daily living activities. At this point in the semester, first-year students have been exposed to the rich, cultural diversity of the university campus. Thus, the ninth session emphasizes tolerance and appreciation for diversity both within the T2U group and across the campus. Finally, the tenth session serves as a concluding event for the fall program. Although this session is the final one for the fall semester, some groups elect to meet informally during the final weeks of the fall semester for a pizza or dinner party.

In the spring, the T2U program resumes during the first week of classes to provide an opportunity for first-year students to quickly reestablish their connection with their T2U group. The spring program uses a format similar to that used in the fall program. The topics correspond to experiences that typically occur in the second semester of the first year of college. The first session serves as a reuniting experience for the group members and also helps to set the stage for goals and expectations for the new semester. Since first-year students may have reconnected with friends at home during the winter break, the second session is an opportunity to revisit those friendships and other meaningful relationships. The students also explore the opportunity to develop new friendships on campus. The topics for the third and fourth sessions focus on campus life; specifically, first-year students discuss their campus involvement and the quality of current relationships. By the fifth session, first-year students are well into their spring semester classes and may benefit from discussing procrastination and avoidance. The sixth session falls at a point in the group's development where, ideally, student leaders are deeply connected with their members and the group process. For this session, student leaders create their own session on a topic specific to their group. The seventh session falls before spring break and focuses on the benefits and challenges inherent in social media use that may occur during the spring break. The remaining sessions follow spring break and are designed to motivate the first-year students to complete their first year and to plan for the future. For example, following the eighth reunion session after spring break, the ninth and tenth session topics focus on supporting first-year students with selecting their major, developing ideas for their career, and making plans for summer and fall registration. Although the eleventh session is the concluding meeting for the group, the students may continue to meet informally for a dinner or a movie night during the remaining weeks in the spring semester.

Format of a T2U Session

Each session follows a typical format with suggested times for each part of the meeting. These suggested times are meant to assist student leaders with the format and timing of each part of the meeting. The five primary parts of each session are check-in, discussion, activity, evaluation, and conclusion. The session typically begins with a check-in that allows time for first-year students to discuss the previous week's events and share any personal issues. This part of the session typically lasts anywhere from 15 to 20 minutes depending on the content and elaboration offered by group members. As the semester progresses, student leaders may allow more time for check-in as group members gain comfort and confidence with sharing more personal details. Following check-in, a discussion of the topic lasts approximately 30 minutes. At the conclusion of the discussion, student leaders then direct the group in an organized activity related to the discussion topic. The session's activity typically involves brainstorming and discussing strategies to assist first-year students with issues related to the session topic. After the activity, the student leaders and group members complete an evaluation of the session. Finally, student leaders conclude the session and introduce the topic for the following week.

Recruitment and Selection of Student Leaders for T2U

In the spring semester of the academic year prior to the start of the T2U program in the fall, upper-class students interested in leading groups may apply for the leadership position. Potential student leaders may also be nominated by those working in multiple offices across campus, including faculty, staff, and university administrators. Interested students complete an application that includes relevant questions briefly assessing the student's qualifications, such as academic record, previous and current experience in other leadership roles, and plans for the future. Following an interview with the program directors, the most qualified students are selected for leadership training (Harper and Allegretti 2018).

Recruitment of First-Year Students for T2U

In August of the first year of college, all incoming first-year students receive an e-mail inviting them to participate in the T2U program. The e-mail explains the purpose and goals of the program and offers information on recruitment opportunities (e.g., location and times to sign up) and participation.

During orientation and move-in weekend, resident assistants, orientation leaders, academic advisors, and other university administrators and staff encourage incoming first-year students to join the T2U program. As early as the weekend before the first week of classes, student leaders recruit first-year students in strategic locations, such as the student recreational center, the dining hall, or other community areas on campus. First-year students may sign up for the T2U meeting time that fits within their schedule. Typically, T2U meeting groups are held in the evenings to accommodate students' class schedules and extracurricular activities. For example, first-year students may elect to participate in the T2U meeting group held on Monday evenings at 8:00 p.m.

Student leaders contact first-year students who have indicated an interest in participating in the program. The student leaders work together across groups to recruit as many first-year students as possible with an expectation that each group will have approximately 8 to 10 first-year students. Once a group is filled, the two student leaders assigned to colead that group will take primary responsibility for the management and coordination of their group.

Initial Contact with T2U Group Members

The student leaders contact their group members to provide logistical information prior to the first T2U meeting. This information includes the group's meeting day and time (e.g., Monday at 8:00 p.m.), location, expectations for the first meeting, and their contact information. Some leaders may use social media to create an online group prior to the first meeting. For example, T2U leaders may create a group chat or Facebook group and send all group members an introductory message.

Leaders' Responsibilities and Preparation for Each T2U Session

Student leaders should strive from the beginning to create an atmosphere of comfort and support for their T2U group. Student leaders should also engage each other and group members by encouraging group members to interact and share information in order to build a foundation of trust and cohesion as the group continues to meet. To ensure attendance and facilitate connection, student leaders should regularly contact group members with reminders of the logistics for each meeting (e.g., time, place).

Prior to each meeting, the leaders should spend time together reviewing the topic and format of the session and determine which role or activity each leader will be responsible for in the meeting. For instance, one leader may take the role of starting each meeting, or check-in, while the coleader may take the logistical responsibility of taking attendance and managing the evaluations for the group members. The leaders should share the responsibility of managing the group so that the group members perceive their student leaders as a team. The leaders should arrive early for each meeting and prepare the group meeting space. The meeting space should be designed in a way that facilitates group discussion (Harper and Allegretti 2018). The arrangement of lighting and furniture should promote eye contact and interaction with each student. To enhance the quality of the experience, snacks and drinks at each meeting should be provided. In addition, attendance and evaluation forms as well as any materials needed for each session should be prepared prior to the meeting (see Appendices A and B). Student leaders should keep a folder for the evaluation and attendance forms. Student leaders should also write notes after each meeting to process the dynamics of the group and note important information to review at the next T2U meeting.

CHAPTER 2

Training and Supervision

The demands and responsibilities of a peer-based student support group such as those in the T2U program can be challenging for the novice student leader. Although strong social skills and an engaging personality are important characteristics, student leaders require guidance in order to connect with group members and create a cohesive and supportive group experience. As such, training and supervision of the student leaders throughout the program are essential for the experience to be successful. The training and supervision program should include three components in order to fully support student leaders in the T2U program throughout the academic year (Harper and Allegretti 2015, 2018). First, student leaders participate as group members in a process group and learn by an *in vivo* experience. Second, student leaders participate in an advanced undergraduate discussion seminar on group dynamics and leadership training. Third, student leaders participate in group supervision about their weekly peer support group in the T2U program. In group supervision, the student leaders summarize significant aspects of their peer group experience each week and discuss strategies for resolving any group-related issues that may arise in the peer group. The following is a description of a practicum course in group dynamics and leadership (Harper and Allegretti 2015, 2018). Student leaders in the T2U program are required to participate in this practicum course each semester.

Course Goals and Objectives

The course is an advanced-level lecture, discussion, and applied experiential course that focuses on the basic concepts, principles, and theories related to group process, group dynamics, and development of leadership skills. In addition, the course includes opportunities for enhancing skills related to the social sciences, including data collection and management using a statistical analysis program, and conducting focus groups. The primary objective of the course is to provide student leaders with an appreciation of the many facets of group dynamics. On completion of this course, student leaders should demonstrate a basic understanding of a wide array of group dynamics topics, such as group formation, group process, and group change. In addition, student leaders have the opportunity to develop their leadership skills in the applied practicum experience, the T2U program. For instructional content, this course relies on the companion book, *Transition to Success: Training Students to Lead Peer Groups in Higher Education* (Harper and Allegretti 2018). This book outlines the essentials of group dynamics, reviews common group experiences and challenges, and also provides techniques for how to facilitate peer groups. In addition, as a part of this course, there are assigned readings that relate to the T2U discussion topics or related content on group dynamics and leadership. Finally, student leaders are required to complete written assignments related to group dynamics and group process.

Part 1: The Process Group

As part of the training, student leaders participate in a group process experience that is facilitated by the program director. Each of these small group meetings occurs in an unstructured group setting. "Unstructured" means there is no concrete task for the group to accomplish. The members do not "have" to do anything in particular; rather, whatever the group wants to talk about or do is the group's decision. The program director facilitates the group process and flow of discussion. As a result, student leaders have the opportunity to learn behaviors and techniques associated with group dynamics and leadership through modeling and observation. For example, when a student leader misses a session, the situation offers both the student leader and the rest of the group the opportunity to learn from the absence and consider how it applies to their own peer group. For example, the following questions may be posed to the student leaders to understand the importance of this small change in the group experience:

- What was it like to miss the meeting?
- How did the absence affect the group and your role in it?

- How do you think group members reacted to the absence?
- Ask group members about what happened in the meeting that was missed. Did group members describe the meeting differently? What might that mean?

Student leaders are encouraged to reveal themselves to each other ("self-disclosure"), share thoughts and feelings about how others are perceived in the group ("feedback"), and make observations about the group process ("analysis"). These elements all constitute the *in vivo* learning experience. This kind of group is a good testing ground for those interested in being counselors, psychotherapists, or professionals in other related fields that involve teamwork and group cohesion.

Part 2: The Seminar

Student leaders also attend and participate in the discussion-based seminar. The content of the class seminar is focused on training student leaders in group dynamics and leadership skills (Harper and Allegretti 2018). In addition, the readings and seminar discussion also address normative issues related to first-year student adjustment and the transition to university life. The assigned readings are primarily relevant empirical journal articles, and student leaders are expected to thoroughly read the article and demonstrate their comprehension of the article by critically analyzing the content of the article and applying it to their T2U group. The articles assigned for the seminar correspond to the upcoming T2U session meeting topic. For example, for the week prior to the T2U session topic 5 in the spring: "*What are you avoiding?*" student leaders read articles related to procrastination as preparation. A list of recommended readings organized by session topic is:

Suggested Readings on Introduction to Group Dynamics

Harper, M.S., and C.L. Allegretti. 2015. "Teaching Group Dynamics through an Application-based Learning Approach." *Teaching of Psychology* 42, pp. 345–348. https://doi.org/10.1177/0098628315603251

Harper, M.S., and C.L. Allegretti. 2018. *Transition to Success: Training Students to Lead Peer Groups in Higher Education.* New York, NY: Momentum Press.

Kottler, J.A., and M. Englar-Carlson. 2015. *Learning Group Leadership: An Experiential Approach.* Los Angeles, CA: Sage Publications.

Suggested Readings on the T2U Program and First-Year Student Adjustment

Harper, M.S., and C.L. Allegretti. 2009a. "Transition to University: An Adjustment and Retention Program for First-year Students." *E-source for College Transitions* 6, no. 4, pp. 10–12. http://sc.edu/fye/esource/archive.html

Harper, M.S., and C.L. Allegretti. 2009b. "Transition to University: The Impact of a First-Year Group Experience on Student Outcomes and University Fit." Poster Presentation at the International Conference on First-Year Experiences, Montreal, Canada.

Harper, M.S., and C.L. Allegretti. 2013. "Expanding a Peer-facilitation Program Beyond the Fall Term." *E-source for College Transitions* 11, no. 1, pp. 16–17. http://sc.edu/fye/esource/archive.html

Jackson, L.M., S.M. Pancer, M.W. Pratt, and B.E. Hunsberger. 2000. "Great Expectations: The Relation between Expectancies and Adjustment during the Transition to University." *Journal of Applied Social Psychology* 30, pp. 2100–2125. https://doi.org/10.1111/j.1559-1816.2000.tb02427.x

Mattanah, J. 2016. *College Student Psychological Adjustment: Exploring Relational Dynamics that Predict Success.* New York, NY: Momentum Press.

Mattanah, J., J. Ayers, B. Brand, L. Brooks, J. Quimby, and S. McNary. 2010. "A Social Support Intervention to Ease the College Transition: Exploring Main Effects and Moderators." *Journal of College Student Development* 51, pp. 93–108. https://doi.org/10.1353/csd.0.0116

Mattanah, J., L. Brooks, B. Brand, J. Quimby, and J. Ayers. 2012. "A Social Support Intervention and Academic Achievement in College: Does Perceived Loneliness Mediate the Relationship?" *Journal of College Counseling* 15, pp. 22–36. https://doi.org/10.1002/j.2161-1882.2012.00003.x

Pancer, S.M., B. Hunsberger, M.W. Pratt, and S. Alisat. 2000. "Cognitive Complexity of Expectations and Adjustment to University in the First Year." *Journal of Adolescent Research* 15, pp. 38–57. https://doi.org/10.1177/0743558400151003

Pancer, S.M., M. Pratt, B. Hunsberger, and S. Alisat. 2004. "Bridging Troubled Waters: Helping Students Make the Transition from High School to University." *Guidance and Counselling* 19, no. 4, pp. 184–190. http://www.utpress.utoronto.ca/GCentre/07784guidco.html

Pratt, M.W., B. Hunsberger, S.M. Pancer, S. Alisat, C. Bowers, K. Mackey, A. Ostaniewicz, E. Rog, B. Terzian, and N. Thomas. 2000. "Facilitating the Transition to University: Evaluation of a Social Support Discussion Intervention Program." *Journal of College Student Development* 41, pp. 427–441. https://www.press.jhu.edu/journals/journal-college-student-development

Tuckman, B.W., and M.A.C. Jensen. 1977. "Stages of Small-Group Development Revisited." *Group & Organization Management* 2, pp. 419–427. https://doi.org/105960117700200404

Suggested Readings about the Coleader Relationship

Atieno Okech, J.E., and W.B. Kline. 2005 "A Qualitative Exploration of Group Co-leader Relationships." *Journal for Specialists in Group Work* 30, pp. 173–190. https://doi.org/10.1080/01933920590926048

Atieno Okech, J.E., and W.B. Kline. 2006. "Competency Concerns in Group Co-leader Relationships." *Journal for Specialists in Group Work* 3, pp. 165–180. https://doi.org/10.1080/01933920500493829

Fall, K.A., and T.J. Wejnert. 2005. "Co-leader Stages of Development: An Application of Tuckman and Jensen (1977)." *Journal for Specialists in Group Work* 30, pp. 309–327. https://doi.org/10.1080/01933920500186530

Miles, J.R., and D.M. Kivlighan. 2008. "Team Cognition in Group Interventions: The Relation between Co-leaders' Shared Mental Models and Group Climate." *Group Dynamics: Theory, Research, and Practice* 12, pp. 191–209. https://doi.org/10.1037/1089-2699.12.3.191

Miles, J.R., and D.M. Kivlighan. 2010. "Co-leader Similarity and Group Climate in Group Interventions: Testing the Co-leadership, Team

Cognition-team Diversity Model." *Group Dynamics: Theory, Research, and Practice* 14, pp. 114–122. https://doi.org/10.1037/a0017503

Nosko, A., and R. Wallace. 1997. "Female/Male Co-leadership in Groups." *Social Work with Groups* 20, no. 2, pp. 3–16. https://doi.org/10.1300/J009v20n02_02

Suggested Readings on Deciding College Major

Bullock-Yowell, E., A.E. McConnell, and E.A. Schedin. 2014. "Decided and Undecided Students: Career Self-efficacy, Negative Thinking, and Decision-making Difficulties." *NACADA* 34, pp. 22–34. https://doi.org/10.12930/NACADA-13-016

Freedman, L. 2013. "The Developmental Disconnect in Choosing a Major: Why Institutions Should Prohibit Choice Until Second Year." *The Mentor: An Academic Advising Journal.* https://dus.psu.edu/mentor/2013/06/disconnect-choosing-major/

Suggested Readings on Romantic Relationships in College

Braithwaite, S.R., R. Delevi, and F.D. Fincham. 2010. "Romantic Relationships and the Physical and Mental Health of College Students." *Personal Relationships* 17, pp. 1–12.

Braithwaite, S.R., N.M. Lambert, F.D. Fincham, and K. Pasley. 2010. "Does College-based Relationship Education Decrease Extra-dyadic Involvement in Relationships?" *Journal of Family Psychology* 24, pp. 740–745.

Grello, C.M., D.P. Welsh, and M.S. Harper. 2006. "No Strings Attached: The Nature of Casual Sex in College Students." *Journal of Sex Research* 43, pp. 255–267. https://doi.org/10.1080/00224490609552324

Jaramillo-Seirra, A.L., and K.R. Allen. 2013. "Who Pays after the First Date? Young Men's Discourses of the Male-provider Role." *Psychology of Men & Masculinity* 14, pp. 389–399. https://doi.org/10.1037/a0030603

Tomsich, E.A., L.M. Schiable, C.M. Rennison, and A.R. Gover. 2013. "Violent Victimization and Hooking up among Strangers and

Acquaintances on an Urban Campus: An Exploratory Study." *Criminal Justice Studies: A Critical Journal of Crime, Law, and Society* 26, pp. 433–454. https://doi.org/10.1080/1478601X.2013.842564

Suggested Readings on Procrastination

Alexander, E.S., and A.J. Onwuegbuzie. 2007. "Academic Procrastination and the Role of Hope as a Coping Strategy." *Personality and Individual Differences* 42, pp. 1301–1310. https://doi.org/10.1016/j.paid.2006.10.008

Chun Chu, A.H., and J.N. Choi. 2005. "Rethinking Procrastination: Positive Effects of "Active" Procrastination Behaviors on Attitudes and Performance." *Journal of Social Psychology* 145, pp. 245–264. https://doi.org/10.3200/socp.145.3.245-264

Krause, K., and A.M. Freund. 2014. "How to Beat Procrastination: The Role of Goal Focus." *European Psychologist* 19, pp. 132–144. https://doi.org/10.1027/1016-9040/a000153

Part 3: The Applied Practicum Experience (T2U) and Group Supervision

The student leader's primary responsibility and focus for each semester is the practicum experience as a T2U group coleader. The student leaders are warned that they should not presume that they are already adept at leading merely because they possess adequate social skills or a confident personality. While social skills are advantageous for this responsibility, the skill that differentiates the student leaders from being merely a peer role model to being a *student leader* is the ability to be empathetic and nonjudgmental while simultaneously leading a group discussion and promoting cohesion. The student leaders are informed that how they act outside of the classroom and group meetings is just as important as their behavior within the group setting. The student leaders are required to maintain confidentiality, demonstrate appropriate behavior that reflects the role of a *leader* on campus, and manage their T2U group. Student leaders are required to meet once a week for at least one hour with their coleader and T2U group members. Attendance and participation at all of the scheduled sessions are mandatory for student leaders. If student leaders miss a T2U group meeting, they are required to reschedule the missed discussion.

For the group supervision meetings, student leaders are required to present a brief oral presentation to their class about their T2U group. The class collaboratively processes and analyzes each group meeting to enhance not only the next T2U group meeting but also provide examples and suggestions to groups that have yet to meet that week. For their presentations, student leaders may rely on their group process notes. Student leaders are required to write and review process notes of each T2U group meeting. The purpose of writing these process notes is to analyze the process of events that occurs in each group. Specifically, student leaders describe not only *what* happened, but *how* and *why* those things happened. For example, student leaders may outline the sequence of events in the group meeting, the group members' interactions and statements, the degree of participation for each group member, and the differences between this group meeting and previous ones. Student leaders should also evaluate the productivity and direction of the group. Finally, student leaders should describe their thoughts and feelings about the group meeting.

At the end of the practicum, the student leaders write a final analysis of their group process. This analysis is a summary not only of their observations in the process notes, but also of their overall conclusions about the group dynamics. Student leaders should review the strengths and weaknesses of the group and analyze the contributing factors to these strengths and weaknesses. These factors may include group composition, critical events within the group, members' roles and involvement over time, and group development. In addition, student leaders propose one specific recommendation for improving the functioning of the group.

Additional Course Assignments

In addition to participating in the class process group, discussion seminar, group supervision, and oral presentations, student leaders are also required to complete additional assignments that further enhance their learning and comprehension of group dynamics. These assignments include conducting and transcribing focus groups, developing a T2U session on a topic of their choice, and collecting and maintaining data collection throughout the program.

Assignment #1: Focus Group

Each pair of student leaders is responsible for conducting a focus group comprised of first-year students. They are provided with additional training specific to leading a focus group and the prescribed protocol to conduct the focus group. The protocol includes obtaining informed consent, audiotaping the 30-minute discussion, and following the structured list of questions during the discussion. Once the focus group is completed, student leaders are required to transcribe the discussion for analysis.

Assignment #2: Open Topic Project

For Session 10 of the Fall and Session 6 of the Spring program, each pair of student leaders is responsible for creating and implementing a group session on the topic of their choice. To prepare for this group meeting, the pair of student leaders must identify a relevant topic applicable to first-year college students, read and review at minimum two empirical journal articles on the topic, and design a T2U session. The T2U session format includes a check-in, the proposed session topic for discussion, questions to assist student leaders with the discussion, and a relevant activity that offers tips and strategies to group members.

Assignment #3: Data Collection and Management

As part of the applied practicum experience, student leaders are responsible for data collection and management of their T2U group. Student leaders record attendance of group members and collect the evaluation forms completed by their group members at the end of each T2U session. They are also responsible for entering the attendance and evaluation into a statistical analysis system.

CHAPTER 3

The Fall Program

Session 1: Welcome to T2U!

The T2U program begins within the first 2 weeks of classes as first-year students become acclimated to their new life. The purpose of the first session is to introduce first-year students to each other and to the student leaders. At the beginning of the session, student leaders will conduct an activity intended to help group members get to know each other. Following this brief introduction, student leaders will then review a set of guidelines focusing on what is expected of all group members (see Appendix C). These guidelines encourage mutual respect, confidentiality, and a sense of trust among group members. Student leaders will also review the meeting schedule and topics with the group members to familiarize them with the upcoming experience. Student leaders should emphasize that group attendance and participation are essential to building a supportive and cohesive group. Following these introductory activities, student leaders will then facilitate a discussion of group members' expectations about university life and their experiences so far. This discussion provides an opportunity for group members to discuss their first days on campus and expectations for their college life. The session ends with an evaluation and review of the first meeting.

Format of the Session

Welcome	5 minutes
Activity: Getting to Know You	20 minutes
Activity: Rationale of Program, Guidelines, and Schedule	10 minutes
Discussion: Exploring Expectations	25 minutes
Evaluation	5 minutes
Conclusion	5 minutes

Materials

- Refreshments (e.g., snacks, drinks)
- Handouts: Schedule of Sessions and Guidelines for the Group (2 copies per person)
- Pencils
- Attendance and Evaluation Forms

Welcome

As the group members arrive for the first session, the student leaders should offer them refreshments and engage in casual conversation to create an informal, relaxed atmosphere. As the group members choose their seats, the leaders should pay attention to where everyone sits and with whom. Seating preferences may be early indicators of developing relationships or cues of personal comfort with social affiliation and proximity. For example, one student may prefer to sit in a single chair, while another may feel more comfortable sitting with others on a couch. As soon as all of the group members have arrived, the leaders should welcome them and share their previous experience in the T2U program, whether as a first-year student or as a returning leader. Student leaders should also explain that the purpose of the program is to assist first-year students with the transition to university life and to help create a social community on campus. In addition, student leaders should explain their role as mentors and available resources for information and support.

Activity: Getting to Know You

The purpose of this activity is to allow group members a smaller, more relaxed context to get to know a peer. To begin this activity, group members should form pairs and introduce themselves to each other. Then, the pairs should "interview" each other for about 5 minutes each. They may ask basic questions about their hometown, family, pets, summer job, favorite movie, college major, or living quarters. After 10 minutes, the pairs will introduce each other to the rest of the group. The student leaders should participate in the activity as well by interviewing each other in order to model to the group members how to ask personal questions appropriately in an effort to get to know someone. The leaders should begin the introductions so that they can set the tone and ensure a relaxed atmosphere for the introductions that follow.

Additional Activity: Second "Icebreaker"

Student leaders may find it helpful to conduct a second "icebreaker" to enhance group connection. In this activity, student leaders ask the following questions:

- If you could pick a theme song for your life, what would it be?
- Which moment of your life do you wish had been recorded and why?
- If it were the zombie apocalypse, which location would you head to first: grocery store, pharmacy, or hunting store?
- What is your superpower and your kryptonite?
- If time and money were not an issue, what would you do?
- If you could travel anywhere in the world, where would you go and why?
- Who is your favorite Disney character?
- What is your favorite movie?
- What is your favorite band or type of music?

Activity: Rationale of Program, Guidelines, and Schedule

Student leaders should begin the activity by explaining the rationale and purpose of the T2U program. The Guidelines and Schedule of Group Sessions must be reviewed with the entire group in the first session in order to set the expectations for the group experience. First, the leaders should distribute two copies of the Guidelines for the Group that outline important rules and expectations for group members' behavior during meetings (see Appendix C). The group should discuss the guidelines, and then group members should return one signed copy to the leaders and retain the other copy. Second, the leaders should review the Schedule of Sessions that outlines future session topics and anticipated session dates for the group to meet. Student leaders may also want to review the relevance of topics and appropriateness of the sequence with group members. Over time, group members may suggest additional topics as the group moves through the program together.

Schedule of Sessions

Session 1: Welcome to T2U!

Session 2: New Friends and Campus Connections

Session 3: Balancing Academic and Social Lives

Session 4: Relationships

Session 5: Personal Values and Beliefs

Session 6: Welcome Back and Social Support

Session 7: Spring Registration

Session 8: Daily Living and Healthy Habits

Session 9: Embracing Diversity

Session 10: Wrapping up and Staying Focused

Discussion: Exploring Expectations

This session topic is intended to address the initial thoughts and feelings related to the transition to university life. In particular, the topic is designed to encourage first-year student group members to share their expectations about their new school and home at the university. In addition, group members are encouraged to discuss their early experiences since moving to their new home.

Naturally, group members may feel hesitant or cautious about disclosing their personal experiences, especially in the first meeting. In anticipation of this initial reluctance of the group members to self-disclose, the student leaders should "model" by sharing their personal experiences of their first few days at the university. The leaders should then invite other group members to join the conversation by asking a few open-ended questions to the group. For example, the leader may ask, *How are things going for you?* Leaders can expect some silence in response to this initial question and should not jump in too quickly out of discomfort. Instead, they should wait and survey the room to see if any group members appear to be preparing to respond. If the silence remains too long, leaders may step in using the "round-robin" technique. Using the "round-robin" technique, leaders pose a question to one group member. Leaders then ask each of the remaining group members to respond in a sequential manner. Using this technique, student leaders invite group members to share a positive experience that they have had since arriving at the university.

Once all group members have had an opportunity to contribute, leaders may then facilitate the discussion. For example, leaders may ask more specific, open-ended questions about group members' initial experiences and expectations about the semester ahead. Sample questions include:

- What were your "highs" and "lows" of your week?
- How was move-in weekend?
- Which campus events have you enjoyed so far?
- Why did you choose to come to school here?
- What initial problems have you experienced already?
- What are you worried about?
- What classes do you think you will enjoy?
- How are your university expectations different or similar to your parents' expectations?
- What are your expectations of T2U?

The student leaders should maintain eye contact with each other and with the entire group. In addition, student leaders need to be mindful of the time and consider questions and directions that are likely to be the most meaningful to the group. If possible, student leaders should end the discussion with the final question in the list, *What are your expectations of T2U?* To help initiate answers to this question, student leaders answer this question with their own personal experiences of T2U when they were first-year students. For example, a student leader may say, "I was on a sports team and I did not have enough time to meet people outside of practice and class. Joining T2U gave me a separate group of friends."

Evaluation

At the end of the discussion and in preparation for concluding the group meeting, leaders should inform the group members that their feedback will be requested at the end of each meeting. The leaders should explain that their feedback is private and confidential and that there is no identifying information indicated on the forms. Each group member has a randomly assigned number specific to the program to ensure feedback remains anonymous. Leaders will distribute evaluation forms to the group members, who complete them before leaving (see Appendix B).

Student leaders should also fill out their own assessment of the first meeting (see Appendix B). In addition, leaders should plan to spend time together at the end of each group meeting to review the group experience. Debriefing is an essential part of building and maintaining the coleader relationship (Harper and Allegretti 2018), and taking the time to review together allows for evaluation of leadership techniques and consideration for the developing group and coleader dynamics (Fall and Wejnert 2005; Tuckman and Jensen 1977).

Conclusion

After all the group members complete the evaluation, the leaders should conclude the meeting by reviewing the important or common issues discussed in the session. Then, the leaders should introduce the topic for the next session, "New Friends and Campus Connections." Finally, student leaders should make a general positive observation from the meeting and thank group members for their time and contributions.

Session 2: New Friends and Campus Connections

Creating new friendships and connections on campus is vital for easing first-year students' transition to university life. During the first few weeks on campus, first-year students must proactively engage socially with their new community. This task can be especially daunting when they are combating loneliness (Cutrona 1982) and homesickness (Scopelliti and Tiberio 2010; Thurber and Walton 2012) in addition to the normative struggle of balancing their academic responsibilities and independent living. However, efforts in the social arena can be essential to a first-year student's success with the transition. The quality of these new friendships is positively associated with first-year students' overall adjustment to college (Buote et al. 2007) and even first-year student retention (Wilcox, Winn, and Fyvie-Gauld 2005).

The purpose of this session is to assist first-year students with establishing new friendships on campus. At the beginning of the session, the group members will check in by discussing significant events that occurred since the previous meeting. Following the check-in, they will discuss how to meet new people and develop friendships and connections with those on campus. Part of this discussion may include how first-year students maintain relationships with those back at home, such as family or high school friends. During the corresponding activity, group members will explore strategies and ideas for creating their new social community. Finally, the session ends with an evaluation and review of the meeting.

Format of the Session

Check-in	15 minutes
Discussion: New Friends and Campus Connections	30 minutes
Activity: Where and How to Meet New People	15 minutes
Evaluation	5 minutes
Conclusion	5 minutes

Materials

- Refreshments (e.g., snacks, drinks)
- Pencils
- List of Campus Clubs and Date of Campus Organizations and Clubs Fair
- Attendance and Evaluation Forms

Check-In

The student leaders should begin check-in by asking each group member about their previous week. Because this is only the second meeting, student leaders should anticipate that they may need to be proactive and encourage group members to participate. Student leaders may rely on specific strategies, such as the "round-robin" technique and asking follow-up questions to encourage elaboration. First-year students may briefly provide an update on a goal they have been working on, or they may allude to an ongoing issue. Student leaders need to be active listeners and pay attention to topics shared during check-in that may be appropriate for further discussion and problem-solving. Suggested questions to facilitate this discussion are:

- How has your week been? (This is an opportunity for student leaders to listen attentively for cue words, such as "good," and follow the response with an elaborative question, such as "What was good about it?")
- Were your classes what you expected? In what ways?
- What were the "highs" and "lows" of your week?
- Would you like to revisit something that you shared from last week?

Discussion: New Friends and Campus Connections

The discussion topic is first-year students' new friendships and connections on campus. Student leaders may find it helpful to initiate the discussion by sharing a personal story from their own first year of college. For example, student leaders may recount how they made their first new best friend on campus or suggest campus events or resources they used to feel more connected to campus life. They should encourage group members to describe their recent interactions with new friends and how and where they met them. Additional discussion topics could also include how first-year students have been maintaining relationships with those from home, such as family and high school friends. Suggested questions to facilitate the discussion are:

- Tell us about a new person you met recently on campus. How and where did you meet that person? What did you initially like about that person?
- Which campus events have you attended so far? Which event was your favorite and why? Whom did you meet there?
- Are your roommate and living situation what you expected?
- What strategies would you use to follow up with new friends that you have made?
- What campus resources have you used already? What resources would you like to try?

Activity: Where and How to Meet New People

During this activity, the student leaders will provide practical tips and strategies to meet new people. Student leaders should keep in mind the unique makeup of the group. For example, some first-year group members may be athletes and may therefore rely heavily on their organized team and sport to make new social connections. Others may be commuters, and as a result, they may not have the convenience of a residence hall or lounge to meet new friends. Student leaders should begin by suggesting ideas for where and how to meet people on campus. Then they should ask group members to participate in the brainstorming session. Suggested strategies are:

1. Use campus-specific social media (e.g., join a first-year student Facebook group, etc.).
2. Introduce yourself to your neighbor (sitting beside you in class or living across from you on the dorm hall).
3. Attend a campus-sponsored social event.
4. Attend an informational session for a club or organization on campus.
5. Attend the upcoming Campus Organizations and Clubs Fair.
6. Invite someone to walk together to class or get coffee.
7. Invite a classmate to get a meal together after class.

Suggested places to meet new people are:

1. Study groups
2. Clubs and organizations' events (provide a list of clubs)
3. Classes
4. T2U
5. Dining hall
6. On your dorm hall or lounge

Evaluation

The leaders and group members should complete an evaluation of the session. Student leaders should also plan to spend time together reviewing the group process.

Conclusion

The leaders should conclude the meeting by reviewing the important or common issues discussed in the session. Then, they should introduce the topic for the next session, "Balancing Academic and Social Lives." Finally, the leaders should make a general positive observation about the meeting and thank group members for their time and contributions.

Session 3: Balancing Academic and Social Lives

For first-year university students, the first few weeks of their new life on campus can be one of the most exciting and overwhelming times in their lives (Jackson et al. 2000). Not only are they experiencing the freedom of independent living, they are also simultaneously juggling multiple tasks and challenges of their new life. These challenges include organizing time for daily self-care activities, maintaining academic performance, and participating in social events in order to create new friendships and a social community. To succeed, first-year university students must quickly and effectively learn how to manage their time and obligations. How university students use their time, such as socializing (Shim and Ryan 2012), studying (Grave 2011; Plant et al. 2005), sleeping (Curcio, Ferrara, and De Gennaro 2006), exercising (Leslie, Sparling, and Owen 2001), and even working off-campus (Devlin, James, and Grigg 2008), can have a significant impact on academic performance and other outcomes related to well-being. Therefore, assisting first-year students with developing effective time management skills will increase the likelihood of success and positive adjustment to their new university life.

The purpose of this session is to assist first-year students with balancing the demands of their new academic and social lives. The session begins with a check-in that gives first-year students the opportunity to talk about the previous week and their adjustment to their new life on campus. Student leaders will then facilitate a discussion about any current issues or concerns group members have about balancing the demands of their new life. Following the discussion, student leaders will initiate a brainstorming activity focused on time management and other strategies that help students more effectively balance their time and responsibilities.

For example, some first-year students may report difficulty with completing academic obligations on time, and student leaders can offer specific campus resources and other information about academic support. Finally, the session ends with an evaluation and review of the meeting.

Format of the Session

Check-in	15 minutes
Discussion: Balancing Academic and Social Lives	30 minutes
Activity: Brainstorming Strategies	15 minutes
Evaluation	5 minutes
Conclusion	5 minutes

Materials

- Refreshments (e.g., snacks, drinks)
- Handouts: List of Academic Support Resources and Weekly Schedule Form
- Pencils
- Attendance and Evaluation Forms

Check-In

Student leaders should begin the session with a brief check-in with each group member. Since this is only the third session together, student leaders can expect to be directive and encourage each group member to participate. Student leaders may find the "round-robin" technique still useful to ensure each group member has a chance to speak and connect with the group. Suggested questions to facilitate this discussion are:

- How has your week been?
- What were the "highs" and "lows" of your week?
- What tests, papers, and assignments do you have?
- What methods do you use to handle your workload?
- Would you like to revisit something that you shared from last week?

Discussion: Balancing Academic and Social Lives

This discussion is an opportunity for students to reflect on concerns that they may have with balancing the demands in their lives at the university. These issues may include difficulties with managing academic demands while simultaneously finding time to create a social life and to maintain daily living activities. Student leaders may use the following questions to encourage group members to discuss their experience:

- What have your classes and professors been like so far?
- How have you managed your time so far? How much time have you spent studying versus socializing?
- What distractions do you have? How do you respond?
- What do you do when you know you need to do academic work but your friends keep inviting you to hang out with them?
- Do you use a planner or calendar? If not, how do you stay organized and manage time?
- What can you do when all of your assignments are due at the same time?
- How do you cope with stress?
- What can you do to avoid feeling overwhelmed?

Activity: Brainstorming Strategies

During this activity, group members will brainstorm time management strategies for coping with the strains of the competing demands of their daily lives. Student leaders should begin the activity by asking group members how they cope with issues related to time management. The group members can suggest strategies for how to organize their time to help them stay balanced. These strategies may include keeping a daily planner, using effective study methods, planning breaks for socializing, and finding ways to reduce distractions. Student leaders can use the Weekly Schedule Form to assist group members with outlining their use of time (see Appendix D). First, group members should fill in time related to their required time commitments and responsibilities, such as class time and sports practice meeting times. Second, group members should fill in time that is flexible, such as self-scheduled study time, time for exercise, and fun or relaxing activities. Finally, group members should review the schedule to identify any remaining, or "hidden," time that could be better used throughout the semester. Using this strategy can help first-year students gain a better understanding and appreciation for how to balance their time to meet social and academic commitments.

In addition to these activities, student leaders will review with group members the list of academic support resources available on campus including:

- Tutors through the Academic Support Center
- Professors during office hours
- Study groups for individual courses
- Workshops available on campus (e.g., time management, study skills, note-taking)
- Peer mentors for courses

Evaluation

The leaders and group members should complete an evaluation of the session. Student leaders should also plan to spend time together reviewing the group process.

Conclusion

The leaders should conclude the meeting by reviewing the important or common issues discussed in the session. Then, leaders should introduce the topic for the next session, "Relationships." Group members may anonymously write down current or previous relationship issues, conflicts, or concerns to share at the next session. These may involve roommate conflict, parent–child dynamics, romantic relationship concerns, and/or friendships. If group members elect to write down issues, student leaders must be prepared to present or discuss these issues at the next meeting. Finally, student leaders should make a general positive observation about the meeting and thank group members for their time and contributions.

Session 4: Relationships

At this point in the T2U program session schedule, first-year students have spent at least 1 month on campus. Their initial expectations of university life are either confirmed or challenged (Jackson et al. 2000; Pancer et al. 2000), and they may find the reality of university life more demanding and stressful than anticipated (Compas et al. 1986). First-year students may begin to evaluate their new connections on campus and may find that initial commonalities may not necessarily translate into genuine relationships. Specifically, novel situations, such as beginning university life, encourage students to immediately connect with each other for comfort and support in order to reduce insecurity and anxiety associated with feeling alone and in unfamiliar surroundings. However, once comfort and familiarity develop, students may realize that these new relationships are superficial. Students may wish to deepen these relationships and discover shared values, interests, and goals.

The purpose of this session is to assist first-year students with developing meaningful relationships on campus. A key distinction between this session and Session 2 (New Friends and Campus Connections) is the focus on the depth and quality of meaningful relationships, not superficial interactions. The session begins with a check-in to allow the group members to discuss their previous week with the group. Following check-in, student leaders will facilitate a discussion about meaningful personal relationships. Then, during the activity, the group members will discuss a series of relationship scenarios that explore common conflicts. The group will work together to identify appropriate resolutions to these relationship conflicts. The session concludes with an evaluation and review of the meeting.

Format of the Session

Check-in	20 minutes
Discussion: Meaningful relationships	20 minutes
Activity: Scenarios	20 minutes
Evaluation	5 minutes
Conclusion	5 minutes

Materials

- Refreshments (e.g., snacks, drinks)
- Pencils
- Scenarios
- List of Conflict Resolution Skills
- Attendance and Evaluation Forms

Check-In

Because this is the fourth session, student leaders can anticipate that more time will be required for group members to check in with each other. Ideally, the group is transitioning from the Forming stage of group development into the Storming stage (Tuckman and Jensen 1977). Student leaders may identify markers of this transition within their group, such as increased interaction and feedback among group members, more personal disclosures, and more opinions that express individual values and beliefs. Student leaders may also want to check in with group members about any feedback from the previous week's topic. For example, student leaders may ask group members about different strategies they used or ways they were more balanced with their time in the past week. Suggested questions to facilitate this discussion are:

- How has your week been?
- What were the "highs" and "lows" of your week?
- How did you manage your time this week?
- Do you have a personal experience you would like to discuss?

Discussion: Meaningful Relationships

The purpose of this discussion is to explore meaningful relationships in group members' lives. Student leaders should begin the discussion by asking group members to pick one personal relationship that they would feel comfortable discussing with the group. Ideally, this relationship will be a recent connection formed on campus that is currently evolving into a more meaningful relationship. For example, group members may discuss their relationship and living situation with their roommate. Student leaders may also ask the group members what specific strategies they are using to strengthen their connection with their professors or maintain supportive friendships from home (e.g., best friend from high school). Suggested questions student leaders may use are:

- How is your relationship with your roommate? Any recent challenges?
- Describe your "closest" friend on campus so far. What characteristics about your friend stand out to you so far? Do you see this connection developing into a deeper friendship?
- What are your relationships like with your professors so far?
- What strategies have you employed to deepen your connection with friends on campus?
- How have you maintained your relationships back at home?
- How have your relationships from back home changed since arriving on campus?

Activity: Scenarios

For this activity, student leaders may either read aloud each scenario or ask group members to read one aloud to the group. Group members are asked to consider the scenario and brainstorm strategies for dealing with these normative relational conflicts. Student leaders should review the list of conflict resolution strategies and ask group members to evaluate these strategies and to suggest additional solutions not mentioned. Student leaders may also want to consider role-playing these scenarios to increase understanding, familiarity, and comfort with these conflict resolution skills.

Scenario 1

I came to school, and now my boyfriend/girlfriend and I are having problems. He/she doesn't go to school with me here, and he/she is now frustrated and really jealous of my new friends. I tell him/her that it's nothing, we're just friends, but he/she keeps asking about it and won't let up. I'm getting worried that we might break up, because we haven't seen each other in a while. But he/

she is becoming too controlling and always on my case. This is really affecting my ability to make new friends.

Scenario 2

My mom will NOT stop calling me. She keeps asking questions about my new friends that she sees on my social media. I don't understand it.

Scenario 3

My roommate keeps stealing my stuff. He/she keeps saying he/she's "borrowing" it, but I really don't think so. We're too good of friends I guess, I don't know, and normally I don't mind I guess, but it gets really annoying when I come home and I just want a Diet Coke, and it's not there. And I know I had one left, but it wasn't there. And we agreed to the 50–50 rule, we'd split half, no big deal. But the Diet Coke was mine, and he/she took it.

Scenario 4

I don't think my roommate is as clean as I am. I mean, there's a basic level of hygiene we should all have. I'm not that picky, and I don't mind a mess here and there, but you shouldn't have to smell up the room. I try and give him/her hints, like "wow, it smells in here" without coming right out and saying "it's you" but it doesn't work.

Scenario 5

My roommate's boyfriend/girlfriend is always around in the room. He/she is there when I get home, he/she is there when I wake up in the morning. It's like having a third roommate and I didn't expect that.

List of conflict resolution skills

1. Get in touch with your feelings.
2. Identify the reason for the conflict—Who is responsible? Take time away from the person to think about the conflict and plan a strategy to resolve.

3. Hone your listening skills.

4. Practice assertive communication; use "I" statements versus "you" statements.

5. Seek a solution or compromise. Be willing to consider alternative solutions.

6. Know when it's not working. If the conflict cannot be resolved and/ or you are getting angry, inform the person that you need to leave and you would like to talk about it later. Consider using a mediator.

7. Recognize and read nonverbal cues.

8. Remain relaxed and focused in tense situations. Monitor your reactions.

9. Stay focused in the present.

10. Choose your arguments. Tell the person how you are feeling (e.g., "I am feeling upset right now"). Tell the person why you are feeling the way you are (e.g., "Your side of our dorm room is really a mess").

Evaluation

The leaders and group members should complete an evaluation of the session. Student leaders should also plan to spend time together reviewing the group process.

Conclusion

The leaders should conclude the meeting by reviewing the important or common issues discussed in the session. Then, leaders should introduce the topic for the next session, "Personal Values and Beliefs." Finally, student leaders should make a general positive observation about the meeting and thank group members for their time and contributions.

Session 5: Personal Values and Beliefs

One defining characteristic of first-year university students is that they become more independent when making decisions. At this time in their lives, they experience the freedom to explore and challenge the values and beliefs that they learned from their family and community. In the university environment, exposure to peers and faculty in more diverse social and academic settings may have a significant impact on students, resulting in a more positive self-image and increased tolerance for others (Astin 1977, 1993; Pascarella and Terenzini 2005). In fact, peers may have the strongest influence on young adult development and growth during the college experience (Astin 1977, 1993). First-year students, in particular, will find themselves in a social environment with those who may hold markedly different values and beliefs. As first-year students work to create their new home and social community on campus, they may experience normative influences and pressure to interact in ways that may challenge these personal values and beliefs.

This session gives first-year students an opportunity to explore and challenge their personal values and beliefs. The session has several purposes. First, this session provides an opportunity for first-year students to disclose more personal and unique experiences to the group. Because of the timing of this session, first-year students will have had the opportunity to interact with others who may hold different beliefs and behave in different ways. As a result, first-year students may have behaved in ways that could potentially be at odds with their accepted value system. Because of this potential dissonance, this topic of discussion may be helpful. Second, this session presents an opportunity for the group to be challenged and grow. By this time in the semester, the group should be stable enough to tolerate and engage in a discussion about diverse and personal experiences. This discussion may induce characteristics indicative of the Storming phase of group development such as a slight increase in tension or emotive responses from group members (Tuckman and Jensen 1977). Alternatively, the group may move into the Norming stage, in which members discover mutually accepted values and beliefs that enhance the connections among the group members (Tuckman and Jensen 1977). Finally, this type of discussion can normalize and support first-year students who may be evaluating their own personal values and beliefs as new information from their peers and faculty becomes available. Student leaders should be especially mindful to demonstrate respect, empathy, and appreciation for all group members' thoughts and feelings.

The session begins with a brief check-in about the previous week. Following check-in, student leaders will facilitate a discussion on personal values and beliefs. Then, student leaders will conduct an activity with the group using hypothetical scenarios illustrating a variety of normative situations that relate to personal values and beliefs. After each scenario, group members will discuss strategies for dealing with the situation. The session ends with a brief evaluation and review of the meeting.

Format of the Session

Check-in	15 minutes
Discussion: Personal Values and Beliefs	25 minutes
Activity: Scenarios and Strategies	20 minutes
Evaluation	5 minutes
Conclusion	5 minutes

Materials

- Refreshments (e.g., snacks, drinks)
- Pencils
- Scenarios
- Attendance and Evaluation Forms

Check-In

Student leaders should begin the session with a brief check-in with each group member. Since this is the fifth session together, student leaders can expect that the group members will be more eager to participate. As a result, student leaders may want to extend this part of the session. Student leaders may want to use the "popcorn" technique, in which each group member jumps in to check in when appropriate. For example, one group member may begin by sharing about the past week, and when finished, the group member may "pop," or ask, another group member to check in. This technique provides the opportunity for group members to engage directly with each other. Suggested questions to facilitate this discussion are:

- How has your week been?
- What were the "highs" and "lows" of your week?
- How did you manage your time this week?
- Do you have a personal experience you would like to discuss?
- Are you making progress on your personal goal?

Discussion: Personal Values and Beliefs

Student leaders should begin the discussion by briefly introducing the topic and reminding group members of the importance of respect and sensitivity for what is shared. For example, student leaders may say:

Our topic today is on personal values and beliefs. Each of us has our own attitudes and opinions, and each of us experiences the world in a unique way. Our goal today is to learn about each other and what we value and believe about certain things. It will be important to be respectful and sensitive to each other especially given that the topic is very personal in nature.

Suggested questions to facilitate the discussion are:

- What is a specific value or belief that is important to you?
- Has there been a personal value or belief that has been challenged or violated in some way since arriving on campus? If so, which personal value or belief was challenged?
- Have you behaved in a way that has challenged or violated your personal value system since arriving on campus? How did this incident make you feel? How did you handle it?
- What kinds of differences in values or beliefs have you noticed among you and your friends? How do you resolve these differences?
- What kinds of differences in values or beliefs do you have with your parents or other family members? How do you resolve these differences?
- Which influence played a significant role in establishing your personal values and beliefs? Religion, parents, peers, education?

Activity: Scenarios and Strategies

Student leaders should begin by explaining that the goal of the activity is to identify strategies for dealing with common scenarios that may challenge or affirm personal values and beliefs. Student leaders should read the scenarios out loud to the group and invite group members to brainstorm how they might deal with the situation if confronted by it.

Scenario 1

I grew up going to church. My parents still go every Sunday, and I know they expect me to go here. For some reason though, it has been easier not to attend church. I haven't really found one yet, and I don't really have anyone to go with me. I feel bad, but honestly, I think I'd rather not go here and just go back to church when I go home. Last Sunday, I lied to my parents when they asked if I went to church. I do feel guilty because it is something that has been a part of my life for some time.

Scenario 2

My roommate drinks pretty heavily every weekend. Honestly, I don't mind; but, I don't really understand it, and I'm worried about her health. I'm not really into drinking, and I don't really care if other people do. It's just that I'm the one typically taking care of her when she gets home, and it's been almost every weekend. I don't want to come across as her parent, but I'm really not happy with how she's acting. To be honest, I think drinking that much is kind of bad. I'm not sure what to do or how to talk with her about it.

Scenario 3

My friend just met someone online and it turns out he's a lot older. He's already graduated from college and has a job, and we just started our college lives. I'm not sure how I feel about this. I know she's an adult, but it feels kind of awkward in some way because she's going on "real" dates with a guy no one knows.

Scenario 4

I can't believe this but my parents just surprised me about their separation and plan for divorce. I didn't see it coming at all, and it totally goes against everything they've ever told me about marriage. They won't tell me why. I don't even know if cheating was involved or not. I always believed marriage was for life, and that's what they told me all my life growing up. I don't know how to reconcile this with what is happening now. I don't even know how I can trust a relationship to work anymore.

Scenario 5

My roommate is sexually active with a lot of different people. I've noticed that it can be one person one night, and the next night it is a different person. I'm not trying to be a prude, but it feels like a lot to me. I'm just not sure how I feel about this. I don't even know what to say.

Scenario 6

I'm starting to realize the group of friends I've been hanging out with have pretty strong, polarizing beliefs about certain things. In the beginning it didn't really bother me, but lately we've been having some deeper conversations and I realize how different I feel.

Scenario 7

I'm really nervous about going home and seeing my family. I've started to realize that I no longer believe what my family believes. I'm worried about family conversations because I don't want to be stuck trying to explain my beliefs, or arguing with them about theirs. I'm not sure how to tell them I feel.

Student leaders may use the following questions to assist group members with their responses to the scenarios:

- What values are in question in this situation?
- Are these values important to you?
- How would you respond to the situation?

Evaluation

The leaders and group members should complete an evaluation of the session. Student leaders should also plan to spend time together reviewing the group process.

Conclusion

The student leaders should conclude the meeting by reviewing important or common issues discussed in the session. They should also remind group members of the importance of respect and confidentiality given the personal nature of the session topic. Since fall break will be the following week, student leaders should inform group members that they will not have a T2U session next week. Instead, the group will resume the following week to discuss the topic, "Welcome Back and Social Support." Finally, student leaders should make a general positive observation from the meeting and thank group members for their time and contributions.

Session 6: Welcome Back and Social Support

The focus of the sixth session is reassessment of relationships, especially those that offer social support. This session is timed to occur after fall break in mid-October when most first-year students return home possibly for the first time since classes began. By this time in the semester, first-year students commonly have experienced some confusion or disconnect with their social supports from home (Paul and Brier 2001; Rose 1984). For example, first-year students report feeling distant from their friends at home because of their divergent experiences since going to college (Buote et al. 2007; Oswald and Clark 2003).

The purpose of this session is to give first-year students the opportunity to process and reflect on the nature of their old relationships and new social relationships on campus. The session begins with the check-in to give first-year students the opportunity to reconnect with their T2U group since fall break. Following the check-in, the group will discuss their experiences with old friends and family during fall break. After the discussion, the group members will participate in an activity that encourages first-year students to think about their social supports, or "go-to" persons, both on campus and at home. The session concludes with an evaluation and review of the meeting.

Format of the Session

Check-in	15 minutes
Discussion: Relationships at Home	25 minutes
Activity: Who Are Your "Go-To" People?	20 minutes
Evaluation	5 minutes
Conclusion	5 minutes

Materials

- Refreshments (e.g., snacks, drinks)
- Pencils and Paper
- Attendance and Evaluation Forms

Check-In

Student leaders should begin check-in by asking each first-year student group member for a brief update about their week. The leaders should anticipate that the first-year student group members will begin discussing their fall break. The leaders need to be mindful of the time and the upcoming discussion and keep this part of check-in brief and focused. Suggested questions to facilitate this discussion are:

- How has your week been?
- What were the "highs" and "lows" of your week?
- How did you manage your time this week?
- Do you have a personal experience you would like to discuss?
- Are you making progress on your personal goal?

Discussion: Relationships at Home

The discussion topic for this session focuses on friendships and relationships with those from back home. This discussion provides first-year students the opportunity to process any recent interactions with family and friends from home. For some first-year students, these interactions may have occurred in person over fall break. For others, these interactions may occur over the phone or through social media. Student leaders should introduce different categories of relationships to discuss, such as friendships, family, and romantic relationships. Suggested questions to facilitate the discussion are:

- What changes have you noticed in any of your relationships with those from home since arriving on campus?

- Feeling some distance or feeling disconnected from your old friends is normal. Have any of you felt this? If so, what have you done to try and reconnect?
- How have you balanced the demands of your new relationships here on campus with putting forth effort in maintaining your old relationships?
- Is anyone in a long-distance romantic relationship? If so, how has your relationship changed since arriving on campus?
- What strategies have been helpful in maintaining relationships from back home?
- Feeling homesick is also a normal experience here at school. Have any of you felt that recently? If so, how have you dealt with it?
- How has your relationship with your family changed as a result of coming to school and living away from home?
- For those of you that commute and still live at home, how have you balanced the demands of your family life with your new school and social life?
- How have your family and others from back home supported you while you are here at school?

Activity: Who Are Your "Go-To" People?

For this activity, student leaders will guide their first-year student group members through a brainstorming exercise to identify their social supports. Their social supports are individuals or even groups that offer help, advice, and support when needed. Social supports can include friends, romantic partners, family, former teachers, coaches, mentors, religious leaders, and even pets. Each group member is given a piece of paper and a pencil and asked to specifically identify social supports. They can be from home or even currently on campus. Student leaders should assist group members in identifying their "go-to" people by asking the following questions:

- Who are your top three "go-to" people in your life? Are they from here on campus or at home?
- Pick one of your top three. What types of support or help does that person offer you?

- Who are your "go-to" persons on campus? If you had to pick one, who would that person be? How did you meet him or her?
- What are the types of social support that you value? Types of support could be listening, spending time together, offering advice, etc.
- Depending on the following circumstance, who would you call? What kind of support does this person provide you? For example:

1. *When I'm panicked, I call . . .*
2. *When my car breaks down, I call . . .*
3. *When my suitemates keep me up until 4:00 a.m., I reach out to . . .*
4. *When I failed my first test, I called . . .*
5. *When I'm hungry and want someone to eat with, I ask . . .*
6. *When I want to watch a movie, I ask . . .*

Evaluation

The leaders and group members should complete an evaluation of the session. Student leaders should also plan to spend time together reviewing the group process.

Conclusion

The student leaders should conclude the meeting by reviewing important or common issues discussed in the session. Then, the leaders should introduce the topic for the next week, "Spring Registration." Student leaders should ask group members to bring copies of their upcoming spring semester schedule and laptops that may help with the activity and discussion. Finally, student leaders should make a general positive observation from the meeting and thank group members for their time and contributions.

Session 7: Spring Registration

The purpose of this session is to assist first-year students with preparation and planning for their upcoming spring semester. This session is strategically timed to occur before spring registration opens and gives student leaders the opportunity to assist first-year students with navigating the registration process. For example, student leaders may review the protocol for how to register, assist with time management and scheduling issues, and prepare alternative course selections in the event initial course selections are not available. This experience does not take the place of academic advising; rather, it is intended to augment the advising process. The student leaders bring experience and knowledge of the registration process and can help reduce the normative stress associated with it.

This session begins with a check-in that allows the first-year students to discuss their previous week with the group. Student leaders should remember to follow up on any issues brought up in the previous meeting. Following check-in, student leaders should prepare the group for participation in an activity. For this session, the activity is intentionally placed before the discussion to assist first-year students with the practical task related to registration for spring semester courses. Following the activity, the students will discuss and further develop their plans for the spring semester. The session ends with an evaluation and review of the meeting.

Format of the Session

Check-in	15 minutes
Activity: Spring Registration	25 minutes
Discussion: Developing Spring Plans	20 minutes
Evaluation	5 minutes
Conclusion	5 minutes

Materials

- Refreshments (e.g., snacks, drinks)
- Laptop and/or iPad
- Block schedule of available class times
- Pencils
- Attendance and Evaluation Forms

Check-In

Student leaders begin check-in by inviting group members to discuss their previous week. More time is allotted for this check-in since the group is more comfortable and cohesive. Suggested questions to facilitate this discussion are:

- How has your week been?
- What were the "highs" and "lows" of your week?
- How did you manage your time this week?
- Do you have a personal experience you would like to discuss?
- Are you making progress on your personal goal?

Activity: Spring Registration

The goal of this activity is to assist first-year students with the registration process for the upcoming spring semester. Some group members may already have met with their academic advisor and are prepared with a draft of their proposed spring schedule. However, other group members may still have questions or concerns about the registration process, and this activity is designed to help these students with social support and feedback from their peers. During this activity, student leaders will review the proposed spring schedule with each group member and discuss time management issues and other normative concerns associated with the registration process. It may be helpful for student leaders to provide blank copies of the university's block schedule of available class times to outline their potential class schedule. In addition, the use of iPads or laptops may be helpful to access online registration information, such as the university's course catalog or course offerings.

Discussion: Developing Spring Plans

The discussion for this session may focus on a number of topics including identifying and becoming more focused on their major, deciding to be involved in a new club or activity on campus, or taking on an employment position. Student leaders may also briefly review with the group the remaining sessions left in the fall program. Student leaders may also ask group members about their thoughts and feelings about their T2U meetings thus far. This reflection about T2U may offer an opportunity to invite group members to discuss whether or not they would like to continue meeting together in the spring.

IMPORTANT: If there are any first-year students who indicate they ARE NOT returning to campus in the spring semester, student leaders should encourage them to discuss their reasons with the group and offer suggestions to see if any of their issues can be resolved.

Suggested questions to facilitate the discussion are:

- What are your plans for next spring?
- What classes are you planning to take?
- Where do you plan to live? Any roommate changes?
- Have you picked your major? What classes/major are you thinking of trying out?
- Have you met with your advisor for spring registration? What is your relationship like with your advisor?
- Now that you've been here for some time, what activities/clubs would you like to join?
- What career ideas do you have now?
- Are you considering a job for next spring? If so, how do you think you will balance your work and academic schedules?
- Would you like to continue with T2U in the spring? Why or why not?
- Some of you may be going into your athletic season next spring. How will you balance your academic and athletic responsibilities?

Evaluation

The leaders and group members should complete an evaluation of the session. Student leaders should also plan to spend time together reviewing the group process.

Conclusion

The student leaders should conclude the meeting by reviewing important or common issues discussed in the session. Then, leaders should introduce the topic for the next session, "Daily Living and Health Habits." Finally, student leaders should make a general positive observation from the meeting and thank group members for their time and contributions.

Session 8: Daily Living and Health Habits

For first-year students, the increased independence when transitioning from high school to college brings the responsibility and self-maintenance of daily life tasks such as adequate sleep and healthy eating behaviors. For instance, college students are now responsible for making their own food decisions (Deshpande, Basil, and Basil 2009; Marquis 2005), which have been associated with negative outcomes (Anderson, Shapiro, and Lundgren 2003; Marquis 2005; de Vos et al. 2015). Additionally, finding adequate time for sleep is often an issue, and, of the numerous life habits assessed, sleep in particular can play a pivotal role in academic performance (Trockel, Barnes, and Egget 2000).

The purpose of this session is to assist first-year students with the independent management of daily living activities. The session begins with a check-in about the first-year students' previous week and any updates that they would like to discuss with the group. Then, the student leaders will facilitate a discussion about daily living activities and health habits. Following the discussion, the student leaders will guide group members through an activity that assesses their current health habits and identifies strategies for improvement. The session ends with a brief evaluation and review of the meeting. Of note, since there are only two more sessions to follow this one, student leaders should prompt group members about the upcoming end of the T2U fall program.

Format of the Session

Check-in	20 minutes
Discussion: Daily Living and Health Habits	20 minutes
Activity: Stay (or Get) Healthy!	20 minutes
Evaluation	5 minutes
Conclusion	5 minutes

Materials

- Refreshments (e.g., snacks, drinks)
- Pencils
- Attendance and Evaluation Forms

Check-In

Student leaders should invite group members to check in about their previous week. Student leaders should be mindful that by this point in the semester, academic issues may be a primary concern as the remaining few weeks of the fall semester approach. Alternatively, by now group members may feel comfortable suggesting a personal topic to share with the group. Suggested questions to facilitate this discussion are:

- How has your week been?
- What were the "highs" and "lows" of your week?
- How did you manage your time this week?
- Do you have a personal experience you would like to discuss?
- Are you making progress on your personal goal?

Discussion: Daily Living and Health Habits

The purpose of this discussion is to review lifestyle habits or activities of daily living and evaluate whether or not these habits are healthy and balanced. Student leaders may use the following questions to encourage group members to discuss their thoughts and feelings about independent living and their approach to managing activities of daily living. Suggestions for discussion questions include:

- Where do you eat (dining hall, take-out)? How often do you eat? Do you eat enough?
- How frequently do you use substances (e.g., alcohol)? How do you feel about your substance use? How has your use impacted your life or ability to manage other responsibilities (e.g., school, friendships)?

- What about your personal finances? How do you spend your money? Are you saving any money?
- What is your sleep hygiene/schedule? How many hours do you sleep? Do you believe this is an adequate amount?
- How does exercise fit in your life? How do you maintain your physical health?
- How do you manage your time with regard to schoolwork, social time, and activities of daily living (e.g., laundry)?

Activity: Stay (or Get) Healthy

Following the discussion, student leaders should then prompt the first-year student group members to assess their personal health habits by examining their daily living activities. Student leaders should ask group members to choose which daily living activities they would like to review. For example, first-year students may elect to outline their meal choices in a given day and evaluate whether or not their food choices are healthy or adequate. Upon assessment, first-year students may realize that due to early morning classes and sleeping too late, they often find themselves eating breakfast "on-the-go." Or first-year students may not have enough time to eat lunch due to their class schedule and find themselves skipping this meal. Alternatively, some students may want to evaluate their current spending habits and connect that with their available finances and school budget. Upon review, they may realize that the majority of their spending may go toward eating take-out meals, a form of entertainment (such as movies or club admission), or even purchasing alcohol or other substances. In contrast, other students may prefer to review their recent sleeping schedule and sleep hygiene. For example, some students may realize how limited their sleep is and the personal consequences they are experiencing related to sleep deprivation. In addition, these first-year students may recognize poor habits that contribute to disrupted sleep, such as using electronics in bed. After the students have assessed their daily living activities, they should identify any areas for improvement. With the assistance of the group, they should set personal goals and develop strategies to meet these goals. For instance, a student whose goal is to eat breakfast may decide to get up a half hour earlier. Other students may wish to prioritize exercise and may decide to set a time during the week to go to the campus gym or attend an exercise class together.

Evaluation

The leaders and group members should complete an evaluation of the session. Student leaders should also plan to spend time together reviewing the group process.

Conclusion

The student leaders should conclude the meeting by reviewing important or common issues discussed in the session. Then, leaders should introduce the topic for the next session, "Embracing Diversity." Student leaders should remind group members of the remaining scheduled group meetings for the fall semester and to consider resuming meetings in the spring. Finally, student leaders should make a general positive observation from the meeting and thank group members for their time and contributions.

Session 9: Embracing Diversity

As first-year students enter into university life and meet new people, they will experience new and different ideas, lifestyles, and cultures. Some students will see an opportunity for growth; however, others may bring with them misconceptions that may cause anxiety and biases toward diverse individuals or groups on campus. These biases may act as unintentional barriers between the first-year students and others in the campus community. This topic highlights an issue that is significant to the student population at institutions of higher education: embracing a diverse student population.

The purpose of this session is to give students the opportunity to discuss issues concerning diversity and tolerance of others. The session begins with a check-in during which the students may discuss significant events of the previous week. Following the check-in, the student leaders will lead the group members in a discussion about recognizing and considering the perspective of other people and commonly held stereotypes. Then, during the activity, the students will consider scenarios and how they would choose to react in the different situations. Finally, the session ends with an evaluation and review of the meeting.

Format of the Session

Check-in	20 minutes
Discussion: Diversity and Tolerance	20 minutes
Activity: Scenarios	20 minutes
Evaluations	5 minutes
Conclusion	5 minutes

Materials

- Refreshments (e.g., snacks, drinks)
- Scenarios
- Pencils
- Attendance and Evaluation Forms

Check-In

Student leaders should begin check-in by inviting first-year student group members to discuss their experiences during the past week. As a follow-up to the last T2U meeting topic, student leaders should consider asking group members whether they made any significant efforts to improve daily living activities. Since only one more T2U meeting remains this semester, student leaders may also want to encourage group members to use some time during check-in to discuss an ongoing situation or problem. Suggested questions to facilitate the discussion are:

- How has your week been?
- What were the "highs" and "lows" of your week?
- How did you manage your time this week?
- Do you have a personal experience you would like to discuss?
- Are you making progress on your personal goal?

Discussion: Diversity and Tolerance

Following check-in, student leaders will introduce the topic of diversity and culture as the discussion topic. The purpose of this discussion is to assist first-year students with learning more about each other's personal and cultural backgrounds. Student leaders should be mindful of the tone and climate of the group discussion. This discussion is intentionally designed to activate curiosity and to promote education by highlighting the diversity not only of the small group but also of the university campus. Suggested questions to begin the discussion are:

- People are really diverse in terms of their religious backgrounds. Some are religious, others are more spiritual rather than religious in practice, and others are not religious at all. How would you describe yourself?
- People celebrate holidays in very different ways. Tell us about a holiday tradition that is celebrated within your family.
- We all come from different cultural backgrounds. Tell us about a cultural tradition that is important in your family.
- What are positive and negative influences of your cultural background on your identity and development?
- How has your culture impacted you during your transition to university life?
- Which culture have you learned the most about since arriving on campus?

As students share more about their personal and cultural backgrounds, student leaders may address the concept of "pigeonholing" and how this type of stereotyping or classifying behavior can be judgmental and unhelpful. To facilitate the discussion of this topic, student leaders may divide the group into smaller groups of four or five people and ask them to identify shared personal likes and dislikes. For example, first-year students may learn that those in their small groups, including themselves, are all "gamers" or prefer Coke over Pepsi products. Student leaders can then ask the small groups to identify subgroups of people with similar interests that are neutral and do not hold any negative stereotypes, such as groups with similar film or sports interest. As the discussion continues, student leaders ask group members the following questions:

- How did you identify yourselves?
- Do you still feel that "label" accurately defines who you are?
- What are the associated stereotypes of just one label?
- What early stereotypes have you already seen or constructed yourselves within your group? Have you felt "pigeon-holed" by these stereotypes?

Activity: Scenarios

The purpose of this activity is to provide group members the opportunity to brainstorm and propose strategies for how they might deal with normative scenarios related to diversity. The activity provides another opportunity in which the student leaders and group members may gain insight into the beliefs that they hold.

Student leaders read each scenario aloud and ask the following: *What would you say or do if you observe the following?*

Scenario 1

You're standing in line at Target waiting to check-out. You notice that a customer ahead of you is struggling to understand the cashier's instructions and questions. It becomes apparent that the customer does not understand or speak English. Another customer ahead of you is becoming irritable and impatient. He states under his breath in a hostile tone, "You should speak the language if you're going to live here."

Scenario 2

You are waiting in line to pay for your purchases. You notice the young man ahead of you, who appears to be from an ethnic minority group, is asked to present ID matching the name on his credit card. When you are in front of the cashier and prepared to pay for your purchases, you notice that the cashier does not ask you to present ID.

Scenario 3

You are employed as a customer service representative at a local store. Your colleague wears a religious head cover. During a store meeting, the manager reviews appropriate dress protocol and states to the entire group "You are not allowed to wear head coverings during work hours."

Scenario 4

You've noticed over the past few days that your roommate has been a bit more quiet and distant. You reach out to your roommate and check in about how he is doing. He pauses and then unexpectedly shares that he is gay and would like your help in figuring out how to tell his family and friends from home.

Scenario 5

You're walking down the dorm hallway. As you pass a neighbor's door, you notice an ethnic slur written on the white board beside the door.

Evaluation

The leaders and group members should complete an evaluation of the session. Student leaders should also plan to spend time together reviewing the group process.

Conclusion

The student leaders should conclude the meeting by reviewing important or common issues discussed in the session. Then, leaders should introduce the topic for the next session, "Wrapping up and Staying Focused." Student leaders should remind group members that the next meeting will be the last meeting of the fall program. Finally, student leaders should make a general positive observation from the meeting and thank group members for their time and contributions.

Session 10: Wrapping Up and Staying Focused

This session is intended to be the last scheduled meeting for the fall semester of the T2U program and should fall mid-November. Since this session is the last "official" meeting, student leaders should take the time to process the experience with group members. Throughout this session, student leaders should encourage group members to take this final opportunity to discuss any ongoing issues.

The session begins with a check-in during which the students can discuss the significant events of the past week. Following the check-in, the student leaders will guide the students through a discussion of a topic that the leaders have chosen that addresses an issue of importance for the group. The student leaders will then review plans and strategies to finish the semester in a successful and productive way. Finally, the session ends with an evaluation and review of the meeting. Student leaders need to allow for adequate time to process the conclusion of the fall semester program and introduce plans to resume in the spring semester.

Format of the Session

Check-in	20 minutes
Discussion: Open Topic	20 minutes
Activity: How to Stay Focused	20 minutes
Evaluation	5 minutes
Conclusion and Introduction to Spring Program of T2U	5 minutes

Materials

- Refreshments (e.g., snacks, drinks)
- Pencils
- Attendance and Evaluation Forms

Check-In

Since this is the last official check-in for the fall semester program of T2U, student leaders may want to give group members more time to check-in about their previous week. Student leaders will need to listen for topics that may be later used in the Open Topic discussion. Suggested questions to facilitate this discussion are:

- How has your week been?
- What were the "highs" and "lows" of your week?
- How did you manage your time this week?
- Do you have a personal experience you would like to discuss?
- Are you making progress on your personal goal?

Discussion: Open Topic

Before conducting this final session, student leaders should choose a topic to discuss that they feel will be relevant to group members based on their previous interactions with the group. For example, some group members may be struggling with roommate or new friendship issues. Others may be struggling with their current academic performance and experiencing stress around improving their grades before the end of the semester. The student leaders will then guide the group members through a discussion of these topics. Additionally, since this is the last organized session of the T2U program, group members may wish to discuss their thoughts and feelings about the overall experience and their feeling about not meeting again until the spring semester. Following this discussion, group members often request additional follow-up meetings or even plan to get together informally themselves. Student leaders should anticipate these requests and evaluate whether it would be appropriate to do so during the remainder of the fall semester. The following questions are suggested questions for the potential topics that the student leaders may choose for the discussion:

- Daily Living Activities: How balanced is your daily routine (e.g., eating, sleeping, exercising, etc.)?
- Academics: How do you plan to maintain or improve your grades in the next few weeks remaining in the semester?
- Relationships: How are your relationships with your roommate and new friends? How have your relationships with your family and friends from home changed?

- T2U Fall Program: This is the last time this semester we'll be meeting together as a group. How does that feel? Was T2U what you expected? What did you enjoy the most? What did you enjoy the least? What surprised you about it? How useful has the group been for you?
- T2U Spring Program: If you plan to participate in T2U in the spring, what would you like the group to do differently? What would you like to continue to have next semester? Do you have any suggestions on how to improve the program? Do you have any recommendations for topics to discuss next semester?

Activity: *How to Stay Focused*

The purpose of this activity is to motivate group members to finish the semester in a positive and productive manner. Student leaders should begin the activity by asking group members the following questions about the topics not covered this session in the previous discussion:

- What are your goals for the remaining weeks of the semester?
- Have you used any of the campus services, such as tutoring? Are there campus resources you would like to use to assist you with your final projects?
- Do you have any conversations that you need to have before school ends? Is there anything you have been avoiding lately?
- Do you need to revise your time to balance schoolwork, social time, and activities of daily living (e.g., laundry)?
- Is there anything you would like to do before the end of the semester?

Evaluation

The leaders and group members should complete an evaluation of the session. Student leaders should also plan to spend time together reviewing the group process.

Conclusion and Introduction to Next Semester

The student leaders should conclude the meeting by reviewing important or common issues discussed in the session. At this time they may invite students for an informal gathering, such as a pizza party, the follow-ing week. Student leaders should also confirm any group members who would like to resume meeting next spring. Finally, student leaders should make a general positive observation from the meeting and thank group members for their time and contributions.

CHAPTER 4

The Spring Program

Session 1: Reunion

As the spring semester begins, first-year students may struggle with their reintegration into their campus life after spending time at home. The first session of the program is held during the first week of the spring semester in order to reacquaint the first-year students with the fall group members. In addition, the spring program is an opportunity to recruit new group members who did not participate in the fall or who may be recent transfers to the university.

The purpose of this first session is to set the stage for the spring program of T2U. At the beginning of the session, student leaders should review the rationale of the program, the guidelines (see Appendix C), and the schedule of sessions. Following this activity, the student leaders should encourage group members to reconnect with each other by discussing their experiences over the winter break. In addition, new members may participate in the discussion by introducing themselves to the group. For the second activity, the group members will set goals for the spring semester. The session ends with an evaluation and review of the session.

Format of the Session

Welcome	5 minutes
Activity: Rationale of the Program, Guidelines, and Schedule	10 minutes
Discussion: Reunion	30 minutes
Activity: Goals for the Spring Semester	15 minutes
Evaluation	5 minutes
Conclusion	5 minutes

Materials

- Refreshments (e.g., snacks, drinks)
- Handouts: Schedule of Sessions and Guidelines of the Group (2 copies per person)
- Pencils
- Attendance and Evaluation forms

Welcome

Upon arrival, student leaders should welcome group members and offer refreshments. When everyone is present and seated, the student leaders will welcome the group as a whole and briefly explain their personal interest and role in continuing the T2U program. The student leaders should remind the group members of how to contact them.

Activity: Rationale of Program, Guidelines, and Schedule

Following the greeting, student leaders will begin the meeting by reviewing the guidelines for the group (see Appendix C). These guidelines outline important rules and expectations for conduct and engagement during group meetings. These guidelines address respect for other group members, equal time for participation, punctuality and attendance, use of electronics, and confidentiality. As the student leaders discuss these guidelines, they should emphasize that group members cannot benefit from the experience if they do not attend meetings. Moreover, the groups rely on the attendance of all members to provide a supportive atmosphere. Regular participation becomes particularly important as the semester progresses and students' schedules become busier. Student leaders should also emphasize confidentiality within the group. This topic should be revisited throughout the semester as a reminder that establishing confidentiality is essential to the success of the group experience. Group members are encouraged to discuss and revise guidelines according to the specific needs of the group. Group members then sign the final version of the guidelines for the group and retain the other copy.

Student leaders also should review the Schedule of Sessions for the spring semester. The topics are designed with the first-year student in mind and address important issues that occur specifically during the second semester of the first year of university life.

Schedule of Sessions

Session 1: Reunion
Session 2: Friendships
Session 3: Getting Involved on Campus
Session 4: Relationships
Session 5: What Are You Avoiding?
Session 6: Open Topic
Session 7: Social Media and Spring Break Plans
Session 8: Welcome Back—How to End Strong!
Session 9: Choosing Your Major and Career
Session 10: Looking Ahead—Summer/Fall Registration
Session 11: Looking Back

Discussion: Reunion

Student leaders should engage group members in an open-ended discussion designed to reunite group members with each other. Topics to consider for this discussion are:

- Recognizing the family dynamics at home during the holiday break
- Reconnecting with friends from home compared to staying connected with friends from college
- Creating new friendships/relationships with those on campus
- Describing new roommate situations
- Evaluating new classes
- Comparing the expectations for this semester to the realities of last fall.

In addition to the discussion, student leaders can suggest ideas and strategies to assist their group members with starting the spring semester. For example, student leaders can advise group members to begin class assignments early and prioritize time management skills. A specific recommendation may be for group members to spend time reviewing class syllabi and marking important dates, such as exam dates, on their personal calendar as soon as possible. Additional recommendations are to prioritize attendance, to focus in class on taking good notes, and to complete all of the assigned reading. During this exercise, students should focus on learning to evaluate the amount of time necessary to complete course assignments.

Improving study habits is another important issue for the leaders to discuss with group members. For example, student leaders can facilitate a group discussion about study settings that maximize the students' focus and attention. In their discussion, student leaders can outline the distractions associated with studying in their dorm room, such as the proximity of their bed, the ease of watching Netflix or playing video games, or the social appeal of spending time with roommates. As alternatives to studying in dorm rooms, student leaders and group members may suggest additional study spaces such as private study rooms, coffee shops, and libraries.

Finally, student leaders can review daily living habits, such as strategies to ensure adequate sleep, healthy eating habits, and exercise. During this discussion, the student leaders should ask the group members to reflect on their daily living habits from the previous fall semester and winter break. This discussion topic may assist with the activity of identifying specific goals for the spring semester.

Activity: Goals for the Spring Semester

The activity for this session is setting goals for the spring semester. Group members generate ideas of goals they would like to accomplish over the course of the semester. Student leaders should ask group members if they are willing to check in about the progress of their goals throughout the T2U program. Examples of goals are:

- Improving grades this semester
- Changing specific behaviors (e.g., reducing excessive substance use, increasing time spent in library)
- Visiting new places on campus or in the community
- Making new friends
- Taking on a leadership role on campus (e.g., residence assistant, orientation leader, peer tutor, etc.)
- Getting a job or internship.

Evaluation

The leaders and group members should complete an evaluation of the session. Student leaders should also plan to spend time together reviewing the group process.

Conclusion

The student leaders should conclude the meeting by reviewing important or common issues discussed in the session. Then, student leaders should introduce the upcoming session, "Friendships." Finally, student leaders should make a general positive observation from the meeting and thank group members for their time and contributions.

Session 2: Friendships

By the second semester of the first year of university life, many first-year students will have made active strides to develop and deepen their new friendships and social supports (Ishner 2004). Compatible and suitable friends play a vital role in offering companionship and emotional support. At this point in the first-year students' academic year, deepening these new friendships into quality, meaningful relationships requires time, consistent application of social skills, and opportunities for social activities. Putting effort into developing these relationships may result in positive adjustment to college life and may even result in higher student retention (Buote et al. 2007; Wilcox et al. 2005). In addition, students who are more involved in organized activities for social reasons experience less loneliness and higher levels of positive friendship quality (Bohert, Aikins, and Edidin 2007).

The purpose of this session is to assist first-year students in developing new and meaningful social connections on campus. Student leaders will begin with a check-in about the previous week. Student leaders will then facilitate a discussion about their group members' current friendships and relationships with a primary focus on campus-based relationships. Following the discussion, the group members will participate in an activity in which they learn strategies for how they can enhance and maintain these new relationships. Finally, the session ends with an evaluation and review of the meeting.

Format of the Session

Check-in	15 minutes
Discussion: Friendships	30 minutes
Activity: How to Make a New Friend	15 minutes
Evaluation	5 minutes
Conclusion	5 minutes

Materials

- Refreshments (e.g., snacks, drinks)
- Pencils
- Attendance and Evaluation Forms

Check-In

During check-in the group members have the opportunity to share their thoughts and feelings about the previous week. Student leaders may provide a model for the group members in order to begin the discussion by talking about their own week and describing events from their own lives. Group members should be familiar with this part of the session from their participation last fall; however, they may feel some hesitation and normative social anxiety about disclosing personal experiences from the previous week. To reengage group members in this activity, the student leaders may need to take a more active role in eliciting information from the group members. A helpful tactic for student leaders is to use the "round-robin" technique and ask group members about their week. This approach can be used until the group members appear comfortable enough to initiate discussion on their own. Student leaders may also ask group members about remaining issues from the previous week's meeting, such as progress on their goals. Suggested questions to lead check-in are:

- How has your week been?
- What were the "highs" and "lows" of your week?
- How are new classes going?
- What is it like to be back in your regular routine at school?
- Do you have any comments about the discussion session last week?
- Have you made any progress on your personal goals?

Discussion: Friendships

At the beginning of the discussion, student leaders should invite group members to explore their experiences with past and present friendships. Following this discussion, the student leaders should ask the group members to describe the characteristics of a good friend.

Suggested questions to use for discussion are:

- Who is your best friend? Why?
- Who are your close friends and how many of them are here on campus?
- If they are not on campus, how do you stay connected?
- Do you want to switch friend groups?
- How would your friends describe you? What is your reputation on campus?
- Compare friends at home/past versus current friends here on campus. How are they different or similar?

Activity: How to Make a New Friend

For this activity, student leaders work with group members on strategies to make new friends or expand their friend groups. Student leaders can offer the following ideas to assist group members with these tasks:

1. Say hello to a student sitting beside you in class that you may not know. Try to sit beside them regularly and begin a conversation about the class experience so far.
2. Sign up for a new activity on campus that you are interested in (e.g., an exercise class at the student health center). You will quite likely meet a new person there who clearly has similar interests or ideas. Intramural sports or clubs are a great way to explore your interests and connect with others.
3. Have you met everyone on your dorm floor? If a neighbor's door is open, or you are on the elevator with someone you don't know (but also clearly lives in your dorm), introduce yourself!

4. Colleagues can be friends! If you are working somewhere, get to know your coworkers. You might have a lot more in common than you realize.

Evaluation

The leaders and group members should complete an evaluation of the session. Student leaders should also plan to spend time together reviewing the group process.

Conclusion

The student leaders should conclude the meeting by reviewing important or common issues discussed in the session. Then, student leaders invite group members to consider the next session topic, "Getting Involved on Campus." For example, student leaders may ask group members to consider a leadership position they have heard of on campus and whether or not they may be interested in applying for the position. Finally, student leaders should make a general positive observation from the meeting and thank group members for their time and contributions.

Session 3: Getting Involved on Campus

Student involvement in campus-based activities has been associated with positive outcomes, including enhanced student learning, academic performance, and degree persistence (Astin 1999; Hughes and Pace 2003; Kuh et al. 2008). For example, participation in Greek organizations has been associated with an increased involvement in other campus-based social activities and higher satisfaction with campus social life (Walker, Martin, and Hussey 2015). In addition, student involvement in campus activities has been associated with higher initial career earnings (Hu and Wolniak 2010). Furthermore, even the types of activities students elect to engage in on campus, whether academic or social, can influence career earnings (Hu and Wolniak 2013).

The purpose of this session is to assist first-year students with becoming more involved in on-campus activities. This session begins with a check-in that allows group members to talk about their previous week. Following the check-in, the group will engage in a discussion in which the students brainstorm opportunities for becoming more involved in the campus community. Then, group members will participate in an activity during which they learn specific methods of how to be more involved in activities. Finally, the session ends with an evaluation and review of the meeting.

Format of the Session

Check-in	15 minutes
Discussion: Getting Involved on Campus	30 minutes
Activity: How to Get Involved on Campus	15 minutes
Evaluation	5 minutes
Conclusion	5 minutes

Materials

- Refreshments (e.g., snacks, drinks)
- Pencils
- Attendance and Evaluation Forms

Check-In

Student leaders will begin the session with a check-in. Student leaders should encourage group members to talk about their previous week with the group. Suggested questions to facilitate this discussion are:

- How has your week been?
- What were the "highs" and "lows" of your week?
- Do you have any updates on your progress with your personal goals?
- What social events have you participated in on campus?
- Do you have any new friendships/relationships you would like to discuss with the group?
- Do you have any comments about the discussion session last week?

Discussion: Getting Involved on Campus

Student leaders will begin the discussion by asking group members about current activities that they are involved in on campus. They may also inquire about previous activities group members participated in when they were in high school or at home. Suggested questions to help student leaders facilitate the discussion are:

- What activities were you involved in at home? Why did you choose those activities?
- Which campus-based clubs or organizations have you already joined? Why?
- Which campus-based clubs or organization would you like to join?
- Are you planning to go to Homecoming (or other organized campus event)? Would you want to go together?
- Which leadership roles might you be interested in pursuing?
- How difficult is it to balance extracurricular activities with academics and personal time?
- Have you joined any new activities since we initially spoke about this at the beginning of the semester?
- Do you have any interest in part-time employment or internships while in school?
- What kinds of activities are you involved in outside of campus?

Activity: How to Get Involved on Campus

During this part of the session, student leaders transition from the open discussion to a more organized activity. This activity is designed to assist first-year students with generating strategies to get more involved on campus. Student leaders may offer their own campus experiences as suggestions to encourage group members to participate in these as well. Suggested questions for this activity are:

1. If there is an activity you are interested in but not available on campus, what steps would you take to initiate this activity?
2. If you are interested in a leadership role, what steps would you take to achieve this role?

3. If you are interested in part-time work for the university such as working in campus dining, admissions, or academic tutoring, what steps would you take to pursue this position?

Evaluation

The leaders and group members should complete an evaluation of the session. Student leaders should also plan to spend time together reviewing the group process.

Conclusion

The student leaders should conclude the meeting by reviewing important or common issues discussed in the session. Then, the student leaders summarize the main points of the session and introduce the topic for the next week, "Relationships." Finally, student leaders should make a general positive observation from the meeting and thank group members for their time and contributions.

Session 4: Relationships

A college campus offers young adults ample opportunity to develop new and meaningful relationships. The quality and depth of these relationships may have a profound effect on the students' overall university experience. For example, in the academic realm, the quality of the student–faculty relationship and level of engagement have been associated with achievement outcomes (Kuh and Hu 2001). In the social realm, the quality of the students' relationships with new friends (Buote et al. 2007), roommates (Erb et al. 2014), and intimate partners in casual sexual relationships (Grello, Welsh, and Harper 2006; Paul and Hayes 2002; Paul, McManus, and Hayes 2000) plays a significant role in overall adjustment. These personal experiences may influence the students' perception of their overall quality of life at the university.

The purpose of this session is to discuss and evaluate the quality of current relationships. This topic allows for first-year students to work through any normative relational conflict that may be occurring in their personal lives. Using the group for support can facilitate commitment and cohesion within the group as a whole. The session begins with a check-in to allow group members time to discuss their previous week. Following the check-in, the students will have the opportunity to discuss the status and quality of current relationships. Then, the students will participate in an activity designed to encourage group members to work together developing strategies for dealing with normative relationship stressors. The session ends with an evaluation and review of the meeting.

Format of the Session

Check-in	20 minutes
Discussion: Current relationships	20 minutes
Activity: Relationship Scenarios and Strategies	20 minutes
Evaluation	5 minutes
Conclusion	5 minutes

Materials

- Refreshments (e.g., snacks, drinks)
- Pencils
- Scenarios
- Attendance and Evaluation Forms

Check-In

Since this is the fourth meeting in the spring semester program, check-in will most likely require more time to complete. At this point, group members feel more comfortable disclosing personal information, and they may have more personal experiences to share related to topics covered in the previous sessions. Student leaders should be prepared to be more flexible with time during this segment to allow all group members to share as much as they would like. Suggested questions to facilitate this discussion are:

- How has your week been?
- What were the "highs" and "lows" of your week?

- How are your classes?
- How are your friendships/relationships? (This question could be a primer for the upcoming group discussion.)
- Do you have any comments about the discussion session last week?
- What progress have you made on completing the goals you set in the first meeting?

Discussion: Current Relationships

During this discussion student leaders should encourage group members to discuss current and previous relationships. Student leaders should ask group members to share current relational issues and if they would like advice or support when sharing these topics. Remember, the timing of this session falls near Valentine's Day. Suggested questions to assist with the discussion are:

- Do you have a relationship issue you would like to discuss?
- How would you describe your relationship with your roommate? How has it changed over time?
- Are you satisfied with your friendships here on campus? If not, why?
- How are your friendships on campus different from other friendships you have?
- What are your plans for Valentine's Day?
- If you're not dating anyone, what ideas will you have for Valentine's Day?
- If you have a long-distance romantic relationship, would you like to describe your experience?

Activity: Relationship Scenarios and Strategies

This activity should be focused on helping group members identify relationship issues and strategies for dealing with these issues. Preferably, the topic should be one of personal relevance and suggested by one of the group members. In the event a personal example is not suggested by a group member, student leaders may use the scenarios described below to facilitate this activity. Student leaders will brainstorm with group members about how they would deal with the scenario and if any of them have experienced a similar issue in their own lives.

Scenario 1

I broke up with my high school boyfriend/girlfriend before I came to school last fall. I was sad for the first few weeks, but after making friends and really liking college, it became much easier for me to move on. But then I just saw him/her over winter break and we spent the entire break together. We are now talking about getting back together. I miss him/her so much and I'm thinking it may be worth transferring to a school closer to him/her to make the relationship work.

Scenario 2

In my first semester here, I thought I knew who my friends were going to be. But as the fall semester kept going, I realized I didn't have as much in common with them as I thought. I was relieved that we had a Christmas break. I'm kind of glad for this new semester because I have a chance to get to know new people. But, in some respects, I feel like I'm having to start from scratch.

Scenario 3

My roommate and I were really close last semester and even talked about rooming together next year. However, he/she and I haven't been as close since we have been back to school. He/she is spending a lot more time with people I don't really like because they party quite a bit. Now I'm not sure whether or not I should room with him/her next year. The deadline to request next year's roommate assignment is coming up, and I don't know how to tell him/her I no longer want to live together.

Scenario 4

I'm not currently dating anyone; however, I have been spending some time with this person on my dorm hall. I can't really tell if he/she likes me or not, but I think we are definitely "talking." I wish the signs were clear as to what our relationship status is. I don't know how to bring this up with him/her.

Evaluation

The leaders and group members should complete an evaluation of the session. Student leaders should also plan to spend time together reviewing the group process.

Conclusion

The student leaders should conclude the meeting by reviewing important or common issues discussed in the session. Then, student leaders should end by introducing the next session, "What are you avoiding?" Student leaders should remind group members of the spring goals previously identified in the first meeting. These goals may serve as a useful point of discussion for the next week's topic. Finally, student leaders should make a general positive observation from the meeting and thank group members for their time and contributions.

Session 5: What Are You Avoiding?

University students may avoid a variety of challenging tasks. These tasks can range from avoiding a difficult conversation with a roommate about shared living space to avoiding completing academic or daily tasks. Avoidance of these tasks can often lead to significant negative psychological and behavioral experiences including anxiety, decision fatigue, and procrastination (Fee and Tangney 2000; Tice and Baumeister 1997). Helping first-year students decipher factors relating to their avoidance of the task can be useful in identifying specific strategies for completing the task. Understanding these factors can have implications for devising successful plans and coping strategies to reduce procrastination and avoidance.

The purpose of this session is to give the students an opportunity to identify situations or issues that they are currently avoiding and to learn how to address these issues proactively. This session begins with a check-in that gives the group members an opportunity to talk about their previous week. During the check-in, student leaders should remember to ask questions about group members' progress toward the goals they identified in the first meeting. Following the check-in, the group members will have the opportunity to discuss issues that they have avoided resolving and tasks they have avoided completing. Then during the activity, the group members will explore methods they can use to motivate themselves to deal successfully with the issues. For instance, they may review time management skills. Finally, the session ends with an evaluation and review of the meeting.

Format of the Session

Check-in	15 minutes
Discussion: What Are You Avoiding?	25 minutes
Activity: Tackle It!	20 minutes
Evaluation	5 minutes
Wrap up	5 minutes

Materials

- Refreshments (e.g., snacks, drinks)
- Pencils
- Attendance and Evaluation Forms

Check-In

Student leaders should begin check-in by inviting all group members to talk about their previous week. Student leaders may choose to ask about any updates in group members' personal relationships. The follow questions are suggestions to facilitate the check-in:

- How has your week been since we last met?
- What were the "highs" and "lows" of your week?
- How was your Valentine's Day?
- Do you have anything you want to follow up on from last week?
- What progress have you made on completing the goals you set in the first meeting?

Discussion: What Are You Avoiding?

The discussion for this session focuses on personally relevant topics group members generate related to procrastination and avoidance. For some group members, these topics may include relational conflict, difficulty completing class assignments or studying, or avoiding a conversation with parents about finances. Below is a list of questions to help start the discussion:

- Do you have an issue you would like to discuss?
- Do you have spring fever? If so, how are you experiencing it?
- How are you balancing your social life and academic/work responsibilities?
- What time management difficulties are you experiencing?
- Are you a procrastinator?
- Would you like to share about a difficult conversation you are avoiding?

Activity: Tackle It!

The activity for this session is a brainstorming exercise during which student leaders and group members suggest strategies for dealing with avoidance or reducing procrastination. Specifically, student leaders will assist group members with ideas for motivating themselves to complete necessary tasks. Leaders may use the goals set in the first meeting as illustrations of how group members can tackle difficult tasks. Strategies may include:

1. Assisting with time management by creating a schedule that breaks down challenging tasks into smaller units.
2. Identifying opportunities for immediate rewards following a short-term task.
3. Inviting a peer to work together on a task and scheduling time to meet to do so.
4. Categorizing "To-Dos" into three main lists: Today and Tomorrow; This Week; Some Day.
5. Role-playing a difficult conversation with someone.

Evaluation

The leaders and group members should complete an evaluation of the session. Student leaders should also plan to spend time together reviewing the group process.

Conclusion

The student leaders should conclude the meeting by reviewing important or common issues discussed in the session. Then, the student leaders should introduce the topic for the next week, "Open Topic." This session is an opportunity for student leaders to develop and implement a session protocol that is more specific to themes or issues they have heard within their group. Student leaders should also remind the group members of the remaining sequence of sessions for the spring program. Finally, student leaders should make a general positive observation from the meeting and thank group members for their time and contributions.

Session 6: Open Topic

At this point in the program, student leaders should have a clear sense of how connected and cohesive their group is and also the topics that would be most helpful to the specific needs of the group. The purpose of this session is to allow student leaders the opportunity to be creative and thoughtful with the discussion topic of the week. Prior to the session, student leaders should consider topics that would be most beneficial to the group. Student leaders will identify relevant questions to lead a discussion on this topic and will design a corresponding activity to educate their group members on strategies for dealing with this issue. Similar to previous sessions, this meeting begins with a check-in that allows group members the opportunity to talk about their previous week. Student leaders should continue to be mindful that check-in may evolve into a more extended discussion. During the discussion, the student leaders will direct the group members through the questions that they feel are relevant to the topic they have chosen for their group. Following this discussion, the student leaders will help the group members to develop strategies that they may use to resolve issues that evolve from the discussion. Finally, the session ends with an evaluation and review of the meeting.

Format of the Session

Check-in	20 minutes
Discussion: Open Topic	30 minutes
Activity: Strategies	10 minutes
Evaluation	5 minutes
Conclusion	5 minutes

Materials

- Refreshments (e.g., snacks, drinks)
- Pencils
- Attendance and Evaluation Forms

Check-In

Student leaders should begin check-in by sharing with the group members the slight difference in session format. Since this session is intentionally designed to address a topic of choice, student leaders should encourage group members to share more during check-in. The following questions are suggestions to facilitate the check-in:

- How has your week been?
- What were the "highs" and "lows" of your week?
- Do you have any updates on the progress of your spring goal?
- Do you have any comments about the discussion session last week?

Discussion: Open Topic

To begin, student leaders will take the lead initially to provide guidance and structure to group members given the slight change in the discussion format. Below is a statement to assist student leaders with setting the stage for their group members:

> *Today's discussion may feel slightly different compared to previous discussions. It is not an organized topic from our manual. Instead, we have identified a topic we believe would be helpful for our group in*

particular to discuss. We developed this topic based upon our previous meetings together.

Student leaders should be prepared for hesitation including silence and nonverbal cues that indicate group members are debating whether or not to participate in this discussion. Patience may be especially key here, and attending to the silence may even serve as an opportunity to begin the discussion. For example, student leaders may comment on the silence and begin the conversation by saying, *I am curious about what is going on for each of you during this silence; perhaps, you may be thinking of what to say or share, or perhaps you are waiting for someone to take the lead. Would anyone feel comfortable sharing?*

Alternatively, student leaders may use the list of suggested questions to help begin the discussion:

- What are your thoughts and feelings about this topic?
- Have any of you dealt with this topic before? If so, how did you resolve it?
- Based on what has been discussed, can anyone else in the group relate to the topic? Would anyone else be willing to talk about a similar personal experience?
- Why do you think we selected this topic for our group?

Activity: Strategies

The student leaders should anticipate conducting an activity that facilitates brainstorming strategies and ideas for how to deal with the issue. For example, student leaders may ask group members the following questions:

- If you found yourself in a similar situation, what would you do or say now?
- What ideas or strategies do you believe would have been helpful to deal with this issue?
- (If a previous issue): What do you know now that you wish you had known back then?
- (If a previous issue): What did you learn from the experience and how do you apply that knowledge today?

Evaluation

The leaders and group members should complete an evaluation of the session. Student leaders should also plan to spend time together reviewing the group process.

Conclusion

The student leaders should conclude the meeting by reviewing important or common issues discussed in the session. Then, the student leaders should introduce the topic for the next week, "Social Media and Spring Break Plans." Finally, student leaders should make a general positive observation from the discussion and thank group members for their time and contributions.

Session 7: Social Media and Spring Break Plans

A primary way that young adults stay connected and informed as well as establish relationships is through social media. In fact, social media is so integral in college students' lives that it can have profound implications on their level of engagement in learning (Junco, Heiberger, and Loken 2010), on maintaining social connections with previous friendships or other social communities (Ellison, Steinfield, and Lampe 2007), and even on assisting in their transition and adjustment to university life (DeAndrea et al. 2012). Despite concerns that using social media negatively impacts social connections, using social media sites, such as Facebook, may actually enhance face-to-face, or "offline," social exchanges (Jacobsen and Forste 2011). The increase in social exchanges can be especially helpful to first-year students seeking to expand their social network on campus (Kalpidou, Costin, and Morris 2011).

The purpose of this session is to explore the use of social media in general and specifically regarding spring break. For some first-year students, the opportunity to participate in a trip over spring break may be their first "adult" trip primarily planned and organized by peers, not parents. Many first-year students may have preconceptions or expectations for their ideal spring break. As such, spring break can be a situational risk factor linked to impulsive behaviors, such as increased substance use (Lee, Maggs, and Rankin 2006) and risky sexual activity (Josiam et al. 1998).

The session begins with a check-in that allows time for group members to talk about their previous week. Student leaders may want to check in about the progress of the group members' semester goals that they set in the first meeting. During the second segment of this session, the group will discuss the appropriate use of social media. The context of spring break is used as an illustration to facilitate the discussion about appropriate and inappropriate use of social media. Following the discussion, the group members will participate in an activity involving suggestions and tips on social media use and spring break. Finally, the session ends with an evaluation and review of the meeting.

Format of the Session

Check-in	15 minutes
Discussion: Social Media Use and Spring Break Plans	25 minutes
Activity: Suggestions	20 minutes
Evaluation	5 minutes
Wrap up	5 minutes

Materials

- Refreshments (e.g., snacks, drinks)
- Social Media handout
- Pencils
- Attendance and Evaluation forms

Check-In

Student leaders should begin the meeting by inviting group members to discuss their previous week. Suggested questions to facilitate the check-in are:

- How has your week been?
- What were the "highs" and "lows" of your week?
- Do you have anything that you want to follow up with from last week?

- How are your classes?
- Have you made any progress on your personal goals that you set in the first meeting?

Discussion: Social Media Use and Spring Break Plans

The topic for the discussion is the relationship between social media and a variety of factors ranging from building one's social capital to concerns for personal safety. Student leaders will begin the discussion by inviting group members to describe the social media applications that they use, the reasons for their use of social media, and any privacy or safety concerns that they have about social media. Student leaders should also invite group members to share personal experiences of social media that have been either positive (e.g., networking, connecting with old friends) or negative (e.g., cyberbullying). Student leaders should relate social media use to spring break by asking group members to consider what pictures they would post and why they would post them as well as what details they would post about their spring break plans. Suggested questions to begin the discussion are:

Social media:
- What social media sites do you use? How often?
- Why do you use social media?
- What are positive and negative experiences with social media?
- Describe your relationship with social media. Is it balanced or time-consuming?
- What would you do if you saw a negative comment or post about a friend of yours?

Spring break:
- What are your plans for spring break?
- If you are going somewhere new/foreign, how are you going to be safe?
- What is your spring break budget?
- Are your plans what you expected, or did you have other ideas for spring break?

- What are your thoughts about using alcohol/drugs/sex while on break?
- Should you post online personal details about your spring break plans? Why or why not?

Activity: Suggestions

During this activity, student leaders and group members will brainstorm ideas for how to be safe and smart, both online and while on spring break. Student leaders may create and review a list of suggestions for appropriate use of social media with group members. The following list is an example of suggestions first-year students generated with the help of their student leaders:

- Review your postings and "clean" them up before spring break.
- Don't take social media seriously. To help with this, don't read or post on them.
- Review all privacy settings before spring break. Consider your personal comfort level of privacy versus public.
- Google yourself (use quotation marks). Know what's out there. Remember to check images.
- Think long term, not in the moment.
- Don't discuss or use images including alcohol or drugs in your posts.
- Don't fight on the internet or over text. Watch the negativity coming through your comments.

Evaluation

The leaders and group members should complete an evaluation of the session. Student leaders should also plan to spend time together reviewing the group process.

Conclusion

The student leaders should conclude the meeting by reviewing important or common issues discussed in the session. Then the student leaders should introduce the topic for the week after spring break, "Welcome Back—How to End Strong!" Finally, student leaders should make a general positive observation from the meeting and thank group members for their time and contributions.

Session 8: Welcome Back—How to End Strong!

In this session, student leaders welcome the group members back to campus and the program following spring break. At this point in the semester, first-year students are well into challenging academic courses with requirements that may be quite time consuming. In addition, first-year students may be more involved in extracurricular activities compared to the fall. These substantial academic and social obligations require first-year students to be effective and efficient with their time management and organizational skills.

The purpose of this session is to evaluate group members' remaining goals for completing the spring semester. Student leaders should encourage and motivate group members to focus their efforts on their remaining academic responsibilities and take advantage of campus-based social opportunities. This session begins with a check-in that allows time for group members to talk about their spring break week. Following the check-in, the first-year students will have an opportunity to discuss their expectations for the remainder of the semester and their ideas for how to finish their first year on a positive note. The topics for the discussion may range from academics to creating more of a sense of community and connection with their university. Then, during the corresponding activity, the students will brainstorm and review strategies that may help them meet their goals. The session ends with an evaluation and review of the meeting

Format of the Session

Check-in	15 minutes
Discussion: How to End Strong!	30 minutes
Activity: Quick Strategies for Meeting Goals	15 minutes
Evaluation	5 minutes
Conclusion	5 minutes

Materials

- Refreshments (e.g., snacks, drinks.)
- Pencils
- Attendance and Evaluation Forms

Check-In

Student leaders should begin the check-in by inviting group members to discuss their experiences during spring break. Student leaders may want to start the check-in by talking about their own spring break. Suggested questions to facilitate this discussion are:

- Did anything exciting or unexpected happen over spring break?
- How has your week been since returning to campus?
- What was it like to be home? What did you do?
- What were the "highs" and "lows" of the week you were away?

Discussion: How to End Strong!

The purpose of this discussion is to motivate first-year students to complete the remaining weeks of their spring semester. Student leaders should ask group members to think back to what their ideas and expectations for themselves were in the fall and are now in the spring. This discussion may also be an opportunity to review goals mentioned in previous meetings. The student leaders may ask the following questions to facilitate the discussion:

- What were your initial expectations of yourself for your first year here at college? Which ones have you accomplished?
- Are your grades what you want them to be? If not, what can you do to improve them in the last few weeks of school?
- Are you satisfied with your friendships and/or relationships? If not, what can you do to improve them?
- What are your strategies to complete your goals?
- What are your identifiable markers of success?

Activity: Quick Strategies for Meeting Goals

The purpose of this activity is for student leaders and group members to brainstorm and identify specific tips that may assist them in the remaining weeks of the spring semester. The following are examples of these tips:

1. Focus energy on one specific goal (e.g., improving grade in one class).
2. Outline at least three clear steps for reaching that goal (e.g., scheduling meeting with professor, completing at least one or two assignments).
3. Consider how refocusing your time and energy in one area will impact other areas of your life. For example, if you elect to focus on improving your social relationships, you may reduce time spent studying or focused on academics.
4. Focus on expanding your social network or increasing your sense of community with the campus. For example, attend an upcoming campus event.

Evaluation

The leaders and group members should complete an evaluation of the session. Student leaders should also plan to spend time together reviewing the group process.

Conclusion

The student leaders should conclude the meeting by reviewing important or common issues discussed in the session. Then the student leaders should introduce the topic for the next week, "Choosing Your Major and Career." Finally, student leaders should make a general positive observation from the meeting and thank group members for their time and contributions.

Session 9: Choosing Your Major and Career

Choosing a major can be influenced by a number of factors including benefits and costs (Montmarquette, Cannings, and Mahseredjian 2002), personality characteristics (Jones and Jones 2012), and family and other relational influences (Beggs, Bantham, and Taylor 2008). Although an estimated 20 to 50 percent of first-year students enter college declared as "undecided" (Gordon 1995), other students may select a major before fully understanding their own personal goals and interests. They may not be adequately prepared or knowledgeable enough to make an effective choice for their major and may select a major prematurely (Freedman 2013; Thorson 2005). The result of this premature selection is that as many as 75 percent of undergraduate students change their major at least once before graduation (Gordon 1995). Faced with this challenge, students may need support and guidance.

The purpose of this session is to assist first-year students with their career interests and potential major. The timing of this meeting should correspond to first-year students' fall class registration for their sophomore year. This session begins with a check-in that allows group members the time to talk about their previous week. Following the check in, the topic of the discussion focuses on group members' major and career interests. Then, during the activity, student leaders will give the students tips to help them in their decision-making process. The session ends with an evaluation and review of the meeting.

Format of the Session

Check-in	15 minutes
Discussion: Choosing Your Major/Career	30 minutes
Activity: Quick Tips for Selecting Your Major	15 minutes
Evaluation	5 minutes
Conclusion	5 minutes

Materials

- Refreshments (e.g., snacks, drinks)
- Pencils
- Attendance and Evaluation Forms

Check-In

Student leaders should begin the meeting with a brief check-in and invite the group members to give updates or reflect upon the previous week with the group. Suggested questions to facilitate the discussion are:

- What were the "highs" and "lows" of your week?
- Do you have any comments about the discussion session from last week?
- What progress have you made on your personal goals that you set in the first meeting?

Discussion: Choosing Your Major/Career

The purpose of this discussion is to assist first-year students with understanding and selecting their major and future career. Since some of the group members may be undecided about their majors, student leaders are encouraged to use the description "exploring" rather than "undecided" in order to normalize the evolving experience of the first-year student. Questions that may be used for those who do not know their major or career are:

- What do your parents/siblings/relatives do for a living? How do you feel about their careers?
- How long are you willing to go to school in preparation for your career?
- What career do you know you are not interested in pursuing?
- What courses have you taken in high school and on campus that have piqued your interest? Are there activities on campus that you enjoy? Could any of them develop into a career?

Questions that may be used for those who do know their major or career are:

- How long did it take you to decide on a major?
- What were you interested in doing before you decided on a major?
- Has your major/career changed? If so, what factors influenced the change?

- What is it about your major that gets you up in the morning? What are the challenges? What are the benefits?
- How do you think your major will be fulfilling?
- What are your goals with this major/career?
- How will your major/career influence your personal life as an adult?

Activity: *Quick Tips for Selecting Your Major*

This activity is designed to assist first-year students with how to select their major and career interests. Student leaders should give the group members the following advice:

1. Don't delay—get curious early about courses.
2. Consider your timeline—you can switch majors, but the longer you wait, the more difficult it becomes.
3. Talk with your advisor about careers/graduate school after the major is selected.
4. Be self-responsible! Review the catalog of courses for ideas.
5. Do an internship early! Be realistic about job market/economy after college.
6. Consider a double-major or minor to maximize skillset.
7. Begin networking. Practice your networking skills. Sign up for events and conferences and then go to them.
8. Create your professional brand through professional social media sites. Begin to invest in your social capital.

Evaluation

The leaders and group members should complete an evaluation of the session. Student leaders should also plan to spend time together reviewing the group process.

Conclusion

The student leaders should conclude the meeting by reviewing important or common issues discussed in the session. Then the student leaders should introduce the topic for the final week, "Looking Ahead—Summer/

Fall Registration." Finally, student leaders should make a general positive observation from the meeting and thank group members for their time and contributions.

Session 10: Looking Ahead—Summer/Fall Registration

At this point in the semester, student leaders and group members should be prepared to wrap up the meetings as the end of the semester approaches. In preparation for the conclusion of the academic year, group members may need advice on plans to return home, to find a summer job, to choose a room for the fall, or to choose summer or fall classes. Resolving the normative issues that the group members are facing can help them cope with the transition at the end of their first college year.

The purpose of this session is to assist first-year students with their plans for the transition to summer and fall. This session begins with a check-in that gives group members the opportunity to talk about their previous week. Student leaders should remember to follow-up on any issues brought up in previous meetings including progress on the goals they set in the first meeting. Following the check-in, the topic of the discussion focuses on the upcoming summer and plans for the next fall semester. Then, during the activity, student leaders will explore tips for developing summer and fall plans with the group. The session ends with an evaluation and review of the meeting.

Format of the Session

Check-in	15 minutes
Discussion: Looking Ahead	30 minutes
Activity: Tips for the Summer/Fall	15 minutes
Evaluation	5 minutes
Wrap up	5 minutes

Materials

- Refreshments (e.g., snacks, drinks)
- Pencils
- Attendance and Evaluation Forms

Check-In

At this point in the program, the group members should be adept at initiating check-in themselves. Student leaders may feel comfortable in stepping back from their leadership role and allowing the group members to begin the meeting on their own. For example, a group member may take the lead and immediately begin sharing about their previous week. In the event the students do not initiate the discussion, suggested questions to facilitate the discussion are:

- What were the "highs" and "lows" of your week?
- Do you have anything you want to follow up with from last week?
- What progress have you made on your goals that you set in the first meeting?
- Did anyone succeed in completing tasks on which they have been procrastinating?

Discussion: Looking Ahead

The topic for the discussion is the first-year students' plans for the summer and fall semester of their sophomore year. The student leaders may ask the following questions to facilitate the discussion:

- What are your plans for the summer?
- What are your plans for next fall? What classes are you planning to take? Where do you plan to live? Do you plan to find a new roommate?
- Are your plans what you expected, or did you have other ideas for the summer?
- What will it be like to go home for the summer?
- How do you plan to stay connected with your campus-based friendships/relationships?

Activity: Tips for the Summer/Fall

During this activity, student leaders and group members will brainstorm tips for dealing with issues that may evolve from their summer and fall plans. The following are potentially problematic areas in which the students may benefit from gaining tips:

1. Signing up for dorms
2. Registering for summer and fall classes
3. Pursuing a summer job or internship
4. Managing parent expectations if living at home for the summer (e.g., curfew, finances)

Evaluation

The leaders and group members should complete an evaluation of the session. Student leaders should also plan to spend time together reviewing the group process.

Conclusion

The student leaders should conclude the meeting by reviewing important or common issues discussed in the session. The student leaders should introduce the topic for the next week, "Looking Back." Student leaders should remind the group members that this next session will be the last group meeting of the semester. Student leaders will want to be sure to have adequate time to process the conclusion of the spring program with group members. Finally, student leaders should make a general observation from the meeting and thank group members for their time and contribution.

Session 11: Looking Back

The purpose of this session will be to conclude the spring program. At this point, group members should be adequately prepared for this final meeting as the group transitions into the Adjourning stage of their group development (Tuckman and Jensen 1977). Student leaders should prioritize time for discussion and reflection on the shared group experience.

This session begins with a check-in that gives the group members an opportunity to talk about their previous week. Student leaders will need to be mindful that the priority is not to quickly resolve situational stressors; rather, the focus of this meeting is to reflect and connect across the group experience. As such, the discussion during this session focuses on reflecting about the spring semester. The session ends with an evaluation and review of the meeting.

Format of the Session

Check-in	15 minutes
Discussion: Looking Back	45 minutes
Evaluation	5 minutes
Wrap up	5 minutes

Materials

- Refreshments (e.g., snacks, drinks)
- Pencils
- Attendance and Evaluation Forms

Check-In

Student leaders begin check-in by inviting group members to share briefly about their previous week. Suggested questions to facilitate the discussion are:

- What were the "highs" and "lows" of your week?
- Do you have anything you want to follow up with from last week?
- How are your classes wrapping up?
- Is anyone struggling with preparing for finals or wrapping up final class assignments?

Discussion: Looking Back

The discussion for this session is on self-reflection. This reflection can be related to group members' personal experiences or to the shared group experience as a whole. Student leaders may ask the following questions to facilitate the discussion:

- How do you feel about your spring semester? Did you accomplish what you intended? If so, what were those accomplishments?
- How do you imagine your spring semester could have gone differently?
- Did you accomplish the goals you set at the beginning of the semester?
- What advice would you give incoming first-year students now that you've completed your first year?
- What leadership positions have you considered pursuing next fall on campus?
- What do you wish you had known prior to entering college last fall?
- Did you earn the grades that you anticipated?
- Do you plan to return next fall?
- Do you have suggestions on how the T2U program can be improved?

Evaluation

The leaders and group members should complete an evaluation of the session. Student leaders should also plan to spend time together reviewing the group process.

Conclusion

The student leaders should conclude the meeting by reviewing important or common issues discussed in the session. Student leaders should be sure to conclude the meeting with positive summary statements and thank each group member for their participation, respect for each other, and confidentiality of the group.

Additional Topic: Campus Harassment

Higher-level institutions interested in the T2U program need to consider the needs of the population they intend to serve (in this case, first-year students) and the availability of resources to implement the program, such as student leaders and appropriate faculty to train the students. One consideration may also be the appropriateness of topics that best resonate with the student population. For example, a session topic on dealing with university administrators and other logistical issues may be relevant at one campus but not at another. Another common experience in campus life may be harassment (Fisher, Cullen, and Turner 2000; Krebs et al. 2007; Lee 1998). A session on this normative, yet unfortunate, campus issue may be useful for some institutions.

This session topic is especially ideal to conduct midway through the fall semester when current relationships and familiarity with campus climate have had time to develop. At this point in the semester following a fall break, students are growing even closer to their new university friends. For some first-year students, this time can be exciting as deeper friendships and social groups begin to form and their sense of identity begins to evolve. For other students, however, this time may be difficult and confusing as they continue to try to connect with new and different people on campus. As these new relationships begin to grow, potentially problematic behaviors can occur. One concerning behavior that is common to university campuses is harassment and, in particular, cyberbullying (Kraft and Wang 2010; Schenk and Fremouw 2012; Wensley and Campbell 2012).

The purpose of this session is to advise and support first-year students who may experience a form of harassment on campus. The session begins with a check-in during which first-year student group members discuss significant events that occurred since the previous meeting. Following check-in, student leaders will facilitate a discussion about harassment and feeling harassed by others, whether on campus or online through social media. Part of this discussion includes identifying the multiple forms and roles of harassment. For the related activity, group members will explore strategies on what to do if they experience or witness bullying by others. Finally, the session ends with an evaluation and review of the meeting.

Format of the Session

Check-in	15 minutes
Discussion: Campus Harassment	25 minutes
Activity: What to Do if Harassed	20 minutes
Evaluation	5 minutes
Conclusion	5 minutes

Check-In

This session begins with a check-in that gives the group members the opportunity to discuss with the group their past week and give any updates since the last meeting. Although check-in is suggested to be brief, it is more likely that check-in will be longer and the conversation will evolve naturally into the discussion as group members share about their recent experience and other areas of their lives. By this point in the semester, group members should have developed more of a rapport with one another and are typically more comfortable with disclosing important information about themselves. Suggested questions to facilitate the discussion are:

- How has your week been?
- What were the "highs" and "lows" of your week?
- How are your classes?
- Are there any updates you would like to share with the group?

Discussion: Campus Harassment

Student leaders should encourage group members to begin the discussion by identifying any new friendships or relationships that have formed since the start of classes. At this point, the group members will likely have a more definitive understanding of who their "close" friends are on campus and, ideally, a deeper connection with their college roommate. Student leaders may encourage group members to describe how they have formed these new social connections and their ways of engaging in positive (and potentially negative) behaviors with new people on campus.

At this point, student leaders should transition the discussion to the topic of harassment on college campuses. Student leaders can invite group members to explore their understanding of harassment and whether or not they have been a victim of this behavior. Additionally, perhaps some may disclose that they themselves engaged in harassing behavior at some point in the past. To assist with the discussion, student leaders should define harassment and describe behaviors of bullying (Olweus 1993, 2001). Specifically, bullying is characterized by a person's repeated exposure to unwanted, negative behaviors by one or more persons and difficulty defending against the behaviors (Olweus 1993, 2001). Bullying can take on a variety of forms and may be demonstrated in a number of different ways. These include physical acts of aggression (e.g., kicking, shoving), verbal harassment (e.g., name calling, derogatory statements, false rumors), and, most recently, cyberbullying (Schenk, Fremouw, and Keelan 2013; Sabella, Patchin, and Hinduja 2013). Those who engage in this type of behavior do so for a number of reasons including finding satisfaction in creating suffering in others and needing power or dominance over others. Victims report experiencing a number of negative symptoms such as low self-esteem, depression, fear, health problems, and suicidal ideation (Hawker and Boulton 2000; Hinduja and Patchin 2010).

Group members in the past have found it interesting to learn about the different roles involved in a bullying or harassing episode. Often times, group members confidently identify just two primary roles: the aggressor and the victim. However, Olweus (1993, 2001) proposed that there are a number of roles group members may find themselves in when witnessing or engaging in a bullying episode. Olweus (1993, 2001) identified these roles as:

1. Followers: Those who take an active role in bullying
2. Supporters/Passive Bullies: Those who support the bullying (e.g., laughing loudly) but do not participate in a direct role
3. Passive Supporters: Those who support the bullying but do not play active role or show apparent signs of support
4. Disengaged Onlookers: Those who do not participate in the bullying at all (e.g., watching but no reaction)
5. Possible Defenders: Those who do not like the bullying and consider stepping in to stop the bullying but do not act
6. Defenders: Those who actively step in to stop bullying

Student leaders should ask group members to identify types of harassment they may have experienced. If group members are not comfortable disclosing or are unable to identify an experience to share, student leaders may use the following scenarios to elicit discussion. For the scenario, student leaders ask group members whether or not these are examples of harassment and to identify the multiple roles found in the scenarios.

Scenario 1

You return to your dorm room and there is a derogatory term written on your door/personal message board.

Scenario 2

A friend texts you and says that someone on campus has written a negative comment about your new Facebook profile picture.

Scenario 3

When you speak in class, two fellow students comment loudly in class that you talk "just to hear yourself talk."

Scenario 4

When you speak in class, you notice two classmates roll their eyes while you are speaking.

Scenario 5

Someone posts unflattering pictures of you on their Facebook page and invites others to comment.

Scenario 6

Your friends intensely dislike this one team member on your team. They tell you to avoid this team member. One day this person approaches you after practice with a question, but your friends interrupt this team member and tell her to go away and leave you alone.

Scenario 7

Following a break-up, your "ex" begins dating someone new. Your friends encourage you to retaliate. In fact, your friends offer their support by aggressively harassing your "ex" and his/her new romantic interest.

Scenario 8

While you are asleep, someone regularly comes by your dorm room late at night and beats on your door.

Scenario 9

On a social media site that allows for anonymous posts, you notice several negative comments posted about your friend.

Activity: What to Do if Harassed

For this activity, student leaders may revisit the scenarios used in the discussion and ask group members to identify what they should do if they are the victims or observers of harassment. The following is a list of suggested responses:

1. Confront the person.
2. Tell a person in authority (e.g., academic advisor, dean).
3. Find a mediator (e.g., residence assistant, academic advisor).
4. Ignore them. Try not to react impulsively.
5. Surround yourself with a "wall" of support (e.g., friends, professors).
6. Document (especially if cyberbullying is occurring). Keep track of what steps you have taken, and how things have been resolved (or unresolved). This documentation can help in the event the situation involves legal actions.
7. Do not minimize what is happening.
8. Do not retaliate.

Evaluation

The leaders and group members should complete an evaluation of the session. Student leaders should also plan to spend time together reviewing the group process.

Conclusion

The student leaders should conclude the meeting by reviewing important or common issues discussed in the session. Then the student leaders should introduce the next topic. Finally, student leaders should make a general positive observation from the meeting and thank group members for their time and contributions.

CHAPTER 5

Assessment

An assessment of any program is essential to ensure a program's effectiveness and success. In the T2U program, first-year students and their student leaders evaluate the program throughout the experience. For example, first-year student members and their student leaders complete weekly assessments during each of the T2U sessions in the fall and spring programs. In addition, first-year students complete assessments related to their overall adjustment prior to the start of the program and also at the end of the fall and spring programs. Student leaders also complete measures that assess their leadership experience both at the beginning and at the end of their first semester in the program. All of the survey responses are confidential and the results are used to assess the program, not any individual students.

Weekly Assessment of the T2U Sessions

At the end of each T2U meeting, both the student leaders and the first-year student group members complete brief questionnaires that measure their general satisfaction with each of the components of the session (see Appendix B). For example, first-year students are asked to evaluate how helpful and relevant the structured activity was to them. The group members also evaluate aspects of the group dynamics such as how connected they felt to the group during the session.

The evaluations for the student leaders assess a variety of factors related to coleading groups and relevant group dynamics (see Appendix B). For example, student leaders are asked to evaluate their confidence, effectiveness, and comfort in leading the group. In addition, student leaders assess aspects of the group dynamics such as how connected the group was during the meeting and the degree to which student leaders felt they were part of a team with their coleader.

Longitudinal Assessment of First-Year Student Adjustment

To assess first-year student adjustment, first-year student group members complete an online survey in August, November, and April of the academic year. Prior to the start of the T2U program, program directors send a link to an online survey to first-year students interested in the T2U program. The survey assesses first-year student adjustment including self-efficacy (Schwarzer and Jerusalem 1995), self-esteem (Rosenberg 1965), loneliness (Russell, Peplau, and Cutrona 1980), depression (Radloff 1977), perceived stress (Cohen, Kamarck, and Mermelstein 1983), temperament (Buss and Plomin 1984), and other psychosocial and behavioral variables. In addition, the survey includes demographic and other factors related to first-year student life such as questions about first-year students' financial responsibility and stress, involvement in extracurricular and work activities, living arrangements, and commitment to completing their degree at the university.

At the end of both the fall and spring programs, the program directors also ask the first-year students to complete these assessment measures typically in November and April of their first academic year. These surveys again assess factors related to first-year students' adjustment throughout the first year and include the psychosocial measures from the August survey. In addition to the August measures, the November and April surveys include measures of the students' perception of adjustment to college (Baker and Siryk 1989), support from the university (Wintre et al. 2009), and their match with the university (Wintre et al. 2008). Also included in these surveys are questions about academic performance, relationship satisfaction with roommate and romantic partner, and participation in campus activities. Finally, these surveys include questions that assess the students' satisfaction and connection with their T2U group and leaders.

Longitudinal Assessment of T2U Student Leaders

As part of the training and supervision course, the student leaders complete pre- and post-measures assessing variables related to leadership skill and confidence. The pretest measures are administered in August prior to the start of the T2U program. These measures include demographic questions about previous leadership experience and current involvement in other leadership positions on campus, personality and psychosocial variables such as temperament and self-efficacy, and self-assessment of factors related to leadership such as peer leadership, motivation, and time management. The student leaders complete the same survey following the completion of the fall program of T2U in November.

APPENDIX A

Attendance Form

Names	Wk 1 _/_/_	Wk 2 _/_/_	Wk 3 _/_/_	Wk 4 _/_/_	Wk 5 _/_/_	Wk 6 _/_/_	Wk 7 _/_/_	Wk 8 _/_/_	Wk 9 _/_/_	Wk 10 _/_/_
Leader:										
Leader:										

Group Members: T2U ID# Phone Numbers:

1.

2.

3.

4.

5.

6.

7.

8.

Leaders: T2U ID# Phone Numbers:

1.

2.

APPENDIX B

Evaluation Forms

T2U Student Leaders: Your thoughts are important to us. Because this program is being developed in hopes of helping future students, your input is especially important. Please take a few minutes to share your experience of today's meeting with us. Do not record your name on this page.

Use the following scale to respond to all statements:

1	2	3	4	5
Strongly Disagree				Strongly Agree

1. I feel confident about how I coled this group meeting.   1 2 3 4 5

2. I felt like my coleader and I were a team.   1 2 3 4 5

3. I was able to keep the group focused on the discussion/activity.   1 2 3 4 5

4. I was able to effectively manage the level of emotional intensity of the discussion among the group members.   1 2 3 4 5

5. At times, I struggled to redirect and reorganize the group members back to the discussion.   1 2 3 4 5

6. I feel comfortable with the group dynamics.   1 2 3 4 5

7. I feel comfortable with the group process.   1 2 3 4 5

8. This group discussion was productive.   1 2 3 4 5

9. I felt aligned with my group coleader.   1 2 3 4 5

10. The communication/discussion was open and honest.   1 2 3 4 5

11. I believe this topic was relevant and helpful to the group.   1 2 3 4 5

12. Overall, the group seemed to find the topic interesting.   1 2 3 4 5

T2U Group Members: Your thoughts are important to us. Because this program is being developed in hopes of helping future students, your input is especially important. Please take a few minutes to share your experience of today's meeting with us. Do not record your name on this page.

Use the following scale to respond to all statements:

1	2	3	4	5
Strongly Disagree				Strongly Agree

1. Check-in was helpful to me.   1 2 3 4 5
2. I was able to be open and honest during check-in.   1 2 3 4 5
3. The activity/exercise for this session was useful to me.   1 2 3 4 5
4. I learned a new strategy for dealing with the topic.   1 2 3 4 5
5. The group discussion was relevant to me.   1 2 3 4 5
6. The group discussion was useful to me.   1 2 3 4 5
7. I was able to be open and honest during the session.   1 2 3 4 5
8. I felt understood by my fellow group members.   1 2 3 4 5
9. In general, I felt connected to my group.   1 2 3 4 5
10. Overall, this group experience was satisfying for me.   1 2 3 4 5

Guidelines for the Group

Respect for One Another

You will have many opportunities to give your opinion on different topics. Others may have different perspectives. Sharing these different perspectives will allow us to understand the topic and each other more deeply. During group meetings, please respect everyone's opinion and support anyone who wishes to speak. Everyone should be given a chance to speak about any given topic and be given equal time to offer their thoughts.

Attendance and Punctuality

We understand that schedules are quite busy with classes and activities. Participating in group meetings should not take away too much time from these important responsibilities. However, given how much we hope to cover together, it is important that everyone arrives on time. If you think you will be late for a session or will not be able to attend at all, please contact one of the leaders and let him or her know. If you are unable to reach a leader, please contact another one of the group members.

Confidentiality

We hope that you will feel comfortable enough to speak openly and honestly. To ensure this, we must all agree that whatever is said during the discussions stays within the group and that no personal information leaves this room.

Cell Phone Policy

Please consider turning your cell phone ringer on silent or vibrate so as not to disrupt the flow of conversation. Also, please refrain from answering text messages or checking your phone.

APPENDIX D

Weekly Schedule Form

	MONDAY	TUESDAY	WEDNESDAY	THURSDAY	FRIDAY	SATURDAY	SUNDAY
6:00 a.m.							
7:00 a.m.							
8:00 a.m.							
9:00 a.m.							
10:00 a.m.							
11:00 a.m.							
12:00 p.m.							
1:00 p.m.							
2:00 p.m.							
3:00 p.m.							
4:00 p.m.							
5:00 p.m.							
6:00 p.m.							
7:00 p.m.							
8:00 p.m.							
9:00 p.m.							
10:00 p.m.							
11:00 p.m.							
12:00 a.m.							

References

Alexander, E.S., and A.J. Onwuegbuzie. 2007. "Academic Procrastination and the Role of Hope as a Coping Strategy." *Personality and Individual Differences* 42, pp. 1301–1310. https://doi.org/10.1016/j.paid.2006.10.008

Anderson, D.A., J.R. Shapiro, and J.D. Lundgren. 2003. "The Freshman Year of College as a Critical Period for Weight Gain: An Initial Evaluation." *Eating Behaviors* 4, pp. 363–367. https://doi.org/10.1016/s1471-0153(03)00030-8

Aspinwall, L., and S.E. Taylor. 1992. "Modeling Cognitive Adaptation: A Longitudinal Investigation of the Impact of Individual Differences and Coping on College Adjustment and Performance." *Journal of Personality and Social Psychology* 63, pp. 989–1003. https://doi.org/10.1037//0022-3514.63.6.989

Astin, A.W. 1977. *Four Critical Years.* San Francisco, CA: Jossey-Bass.

Astin, A.W. 1993. *What Matters in College.* San Francisco, CA: Jossey-Bass.

Astin, A.W. 1999. "Student Involvement: A Developmental Theory of Higher Education." *Journal of College Student Development* 40, pp. 518–529. http://www.ydae.purdue.edu/lct/hbcu/documents/Student_Involvement_A_Developmental_Theory_for_HE_Astin.pdf

Atieno Okech, J.E., and W.B. Kline. 2005. "A Qualitative Exploration of Group Co-leader Relationships." *Journal for Specialists in Group Work* 30, pp. 173–190. https://doi.org/10.1080/01933920590926048

Atieno Okech, J.E., and W.B. Kline. 2006. "Competency Concerns in Group Co-leader Relationships." *Journal for Specialists in Group Work* 3, pp. 165–180. https://doi.org/10.1080/01933920500493829

Ayers, J.F., J.F. Mattanah, L. Brooks, J.L. Quimby, and B.L. Brand. 2006. *Results of a Psychosocial Intervention Program to Facilitate Adjustment to College.* Paper Presented at the Annual Convention of the Society for Research on Adolescents, San Francisco, CA.

Baker, R.W., and B. Siryk. 1984. "Measuring Adjustment to College." *Journal of Counseling Psychology* 31, pp. 179–189. https://doi.org/10.1037//0022-0167.31.2.179

Barefoot, B.O. 2005. "Current Institutional Practices in the First College Year." In *Challenging and Supporting the First-year Student: A Handbook for Improving the First Year of College,* eds. M.L. Upcraft, J.N. Gardner, and B.O. Barefoot, pp. 47–63. San Francisco, CA: Jossey-Bass.

Beggs, J., J. Bantham, and S. Taylor. 2008. "Distinguishing the Factors Influencing College Students' Choice of Major." *College Student Journal* 42, pp. 381–394. https://www.questia.com/read/1G1-179348418/distinguishing-the-factors-influencing-college-students

Bohert, A.M., J.W. Aikins, and J. Edidin. 2007. "The Role of Organized Activities in Facilitating Social Adaptation across the Transition to College." *Journal of Adolescent Research* 22, pp. 189–208. https://doi.org/10.1177/0743558406297940

Braithwaite, S.R., R. Delevi, and F.D. Fincham. 2010. "Romantic Relationships and the Physical and Mental Health of College Students." *Personal Relationships* 17, pp. 1–12. https://doi.org/10.1111/j.1475-6811.2010.01248.x

Braithwaite, S.R., N.M. Lambert, F.D. Fincham, and K. Pasley. 2010. "Does College-based Relationship Education Decrease Extra-dyadic Involvement in Relationships?" *Journal of Family Psychology* 24, pp. 740–745. https://doi.org/10.1037/a0021759

Brooks, J.H., and D.L. DuBois. 1995. "Individual and Environmental Predictors of Adjustment During the First Year of College." *Journal of College Student Development* 36, pp. 347–360. http://www.myacpa.org/journal-college-student-development

Bullock-Yowell, E., A.E. McConnell, and E.A. Schedin. 2014. "Decided and Undecided Students: Career Self-efficacy, Negative Thinking, and Decision-making Difficulties." *NACADA* 34, pp. 22–34. https://doi.org/10.12930/NACADA-13-016

Buote, V., S.M. Pancer, M. Pratt, G. Adams, S. Birnie-Lefcovitch, J. Polivy, and M.G. Wintre. 2007. "The Importance of Friends: Friendships and Adjustment Among First-year University Students." *Journal of Adolescent Research* 22, pp. 665–689. https://doi.org/10.1177/0743558407306344

Buss, A.H., and R. Plomin. 1984. *Temperament: Early Developing Personality Traits*. Hillsdale, NJ: Lawrence Erlbaum Associates, Inc.

Chun, Chu, A.H., and J.N. Choi. 2005. "Rethinking Procrastination: Positive Effects of "Active" Procrastination Behaviors on Attitudes and Performance." *Journal of Social Psychology* 145, pp. 245–264. https://doi.org/10.3200/socp.145.3.245-264

Cohen, S., T. Kamarck, and R. Mermelstein. 1983. "A Global Measure of Perceived Stress." *Journal of Health and Social Behavior* 24, pp. 385–396. https://doi.org/10.2307/2136404

Compas, B.E., B.M. Wagner, L.A. Slavin, and K. Vannatta. 1986. "A Prospective Study of Life Events, Social Support, and Psychological Symptomology During the Transition from High School to College." *American Journal of Community Psychology* 14, pp. 241–257. https://doi.org/10.1007/bf00911173

Curcio, G., M. Ferrara, and L. De Gennaro. 2006. "Sleep Loss, Learning Capacity and Academic Performance." *Sleep Medicine Reviews* 10, pp. 323–337. https://doi.org/10.1016/j.smrv.2005.11.001

Cutrona, C.E. 1982. "Transition to College: Loneliness and the Process of Social Adjustment." In *Loneliness: A Source Book of Current Theory, Research, and*

Therapy, eds. L.A. Peplau and D. Perlman, pp. 291–309. New York, NY: John Wiley & Sons.

DeAndrea, D.C., N. Ellison, R. LaRose, C. Steinfield, and A. Fiore. 2012. "Serious Social Media: On the Use of Social Media for Improving Students' Adjustment to College." *Internet and Higher Education* 15, pp. 15–23. https://doi.org/10.1016/j.iheduc.2011.05.009

Deshpande, S., M.D. Basil, and D.B. Basil. 2009. "Factors Influencing Healthy Eating Habits Among College Students: An Application of the Health Belief Model." *Health Marketing Quarterly* 26, pp. 145–164. https://doi .org/10.1080/07359680802619834

Devlin, M., R. James, and G. Grigg. 2008. "Studying and Working: A National Study of Student Finances and Student Engagement." *Tertiary Education and Management* 14, pp. 111–122. https://doi.org/10.1080/13583880802053044

de Vos, P., C. Hanck, M. Neisingh, D. Prak, H. Groen, and M. Faas. 2015. "Weight Gain in Freshman College Students and Perceived Health." *Preventive Medicine Reports* 2, pp. 229–234. https://doi.org/10.1016/j.pmedr.2015.03.008

Ellison, N., C. Steinfield, and C. Lampe. 2007. "The Benefits of Facebook 'Friends': Social Capital and College Students' Use of Online Social Network Sites." *Journal of Computer-Mediated Communication* 12, pp. 1143–1168. https://doi.org/10.1111/j.1083-6101.2007.00367.x

Erb, S.E., K.D. Renshaw, J.L. Short, and J.W. Pollard. 2014. "The Importance of College Roommate Relationships: A Review and Systemic Conceptualization." *Journal of Student Affairs Research and Practice* 51, pp. 43–55. http:// dx.doi.org/10.1515/jsarp-2014-0004

Fall, K.A., and T.J. Wejnert. 2005. "Co-leader Stages of Development: An Application of Tuckman and Jensen (1977)." *Journal for Specialists in Group Work* 61, pp. 309–327. https://doi.org/10.1080/01933920500186530

Fee, R.L., and J.P. Tangney. 2000. "Procrastination: A Means of Avoiding Shame or Guilt?" *Journal of Social Behavior and Personality* 15, pp. 167–184. https:// www.sbp-journal.com/index.php/sbp

Fisher, B., F. Cullen, and M. Turner. 2000. *The Sexual Victimization of College Women* (NCJ182369). The National Criminal Justice Reference Service. https://www.ncjrs.gov/pdffiles1/nij/182369.pdf

Fisher, S., and B. Hood. 1988. "Vulnerability Factors in the Transition to University: Self-reported Mobility History and Sex Differences as Factors in Psychological Disturbance." *British Journal of Psychology* 79, pp. 309–320. https://doi.org/10.1111/j.2044-8295.1988.tb02290.x

Freedman, L. 2013. "The Developmental Disconnect in Choosing a Major: Why Institutions Should Prohibit Choice Until Second Year." *The Mentor: An Academic Advising Journal.* https://dus.psu.edu/mentor/2013/06/disconnect-choosing-major/

Gall, T.L., D.R. Evans, and S. Bellerose. 2000. "Transition to First-year University: Patterns of Change in Adjustment Across Life Domains and Time." *Journal of Social and Clinical Psychology* 19, pp. 544–567. https://doi.org/10.1521/jscp.2000.19.4.544

Gerdes, H., and B. Mallinckrodt. 1994. "Emotional, Social, and Academic Adjustment of College Students: A Longitudinal Study of Retention." *Journal of Counseling and Development* 72, pp. 281–288. https://doi.org/10.1002/j.1556-6676.1994.tb00935.x

Gordon, V.N. 1995. *The Undecided College Student: An Academic and Career Advising Challenge*, 2nd ed. Springfield, IL: Charles C. Thomas.

Grave, B.S. 2011. "The Effect of Student Time Allocation on Academic Achievement." *Education Economics* 19, pp. 291–310. https://doi.org/10.1080/09645292.2011.585794

Grello, C.M., D.P. Welsh, and M.S. Harper. 2006. "No Strings Attached: The Nature of Casual Sex in College Students." *Journal of Sex Research* 43, pp. 255–267. https://doi.org/10.1080/00224490609552324

Hamilton, S.F., and M.A. Hamilton. 2006. "School, Work, and Emerging Adulthood." In *Emerging adults in America: Coming of Age in the 21st Century*, eds. J.J. Arnett and J.L. Tanner, pp. 440–473. Washington, DC: American Psychological Association.

Harper, M.S., and C.L. Allegretti. 2009a. "Transition to University: An adjustment and Retention Program for First-year Students." *E-source for College Transitions* 6, no. 4, pp. 10–12. http://sc.edu/fye/esource/archive.html

Harper, M.S., and C.L. Allegretti. 2009b. *Transition to University: The Impact of a First-year Group Experience on Student Outcomes and University Fit*. Poster presentation at the International Conference on First-Year Experiences, Montreal, Canada.

Harper, M.S., and C.L. Allegretti. 2013. "Expanding a Peer-facilitation Program Beyond the Fall Term." *E-Source for College Transitions* 11, no. 1, pp. 16–17. http://sc.edu/fye/esource/archive.html

Harper, M.S., and C.L. Allegretti. 2015. "Teaching Group Dynamics Through an Application-based Learning Approach." *Teaching of Psychology* 42, pp. 345–348. https://doi.org/10.1177/0098628315603251

Harper, M.S., and C.L. Allegretti. 2018. *Transition to Success: Training Students to Lead Peer Groups in Higher Education*. New York, NY: Momentum Press.

Hawker, D.S.J., and M.J. Boulton. 2000. "Twenty years' Research on Peer Victimization and Psychosocial Maladjustment: A Meta-analytic Review of Cross-sectional Studies." *Journal of Child Psychiatry and Psychiatry* 41, pp. 441–455. https://doi.org/10.1017/s0021963099005545

Hinduja, S., and J.W. Patchin. 2010. "Bullying, cyberbullying, and suicide." *Archives of Suicide Research* 14, pp. 206–221. https://doi.org/10.1080/13811118.2010.494133

Hu, S., and G.C. Wolniak. 2010. "Initial Evidence on the Influence of College Student Engagement on Early Career Earnings." *Research in Higher Education* 51, pp. 750–766. https://doi.org/10.1007/s11162-010-9176-1

Hu, S., and G.C. Wolniak. 2013. "College Student Engagement and Early Career Earnings: Differences by Gender, Race/Ethnicity, and Academic Preparation." *Review of Higher Education* 36, pp. 211–233. https://doi.org/10.1353/rhe.2013.0002

Hughes, R., and C.R. Pace. 2003. "Using NSSE to Study Student Retention and Withdrawal." *Assessment Update* 15, no. 4, pp. 1–2. https://www.uccs.edu/Documents/retention/2003%20Using%20NSSE%20to%20Study%20Student%20Retention%20and%20Withdrawal.pdf

Hunsberger, B., S.M. Pancer, M. Pratt, E. Rog, and S. Alisat. 2003. *Bridge Over Troubled Water: Easing the Transition to University.* Unpublished Manuscript.

Ishner, J.L.C. 2004. "Tracing "Friendsickness" During the First Year of College Through Journal Writing: A Qualitative Study." *Journal of Student Affairs Research and Practice* 41, pp. 518–537. https://doi.org/10.2202/1949-6605.1359

Jackson, L.M., S.M. Pancer, M.W. Pratt, and B.E. Hunsberger. 2000. "Great Expectations: The Relation Between Expectancies and Adjustment During the Transition to University." *Journal of Applied Social Psychology* 30, pp. 2100–2125. https://doi.org/10.1111/j.1559-1816.2000.tb02427.x

Jacobsen, W.C., and R. Forste. 2011. "The Wired Generation: Academic and Social Outcomes of Electronic Media use Among University Students." *Cyberpsychology, Behavior, and Social Networking* 14, pp. 275–280. https://doi.org/10.1084/cyber.2010.0135

Jaramillo-Seirra, A.L., and K.R. Allen. 2013. "Who Pays after the First Date? Young Men's Discourses of the Male-provider Role." *Psychology of Men & Masculinity* 14, pp. 389–399. https://doi.org/10.1037/a0030603

Jones, L.K., and J.W. Jones. 2012. *Personality-college Major Match and Student Success: A Guide for Professionals Helping Youth and Adults Who are in College or are College-bound.* http://www.careerkey.org/pdf/Personality-College_Major_Match_Guide_Professionals.pdf

Josiam, B., J.S.P. Hobson, U. Dietrich, and G. Smeaton. 1998. "An Analysis of the Sexual, Alcohol, and Drug related Behavioral Patterns of Students on Spring Break." *Tourism Management* 19, pp. 501–513. https://doi.org/10.1016/S0261-5177(98)00052-1

Junco, R., G. Heiberger, and E. Loken. 2010. "The Effect of Twitter on College Student Engagement and Grades." *Journal of Computer Assisted Learning* 27, pp. 119–132. https://doi.org/10.1111/j.1365-2729.2010.00387.x

Kalpidou, M., D. Costin, and J. Morris. 2011. "The Relationship Between Facebook and the Well-Being of Undergraduate College Students." *Cyberpsychology,*

Behavior & Social Networking 14, pp. 183–189. https://doi.org/10.1089/cyber.2010.0061

Kottler, J.A., and M. Englar-Carlson. 2015. *Learning Group Leadership: An Experiential Approach.* Los Angeles, CA: Sage Publications.

Kraft, E., and J. Wang. 2010. "An Exploratory Study of the Cyberbullying and Cyberstalking Experiences and Factors Related to Victimization of Students at a Public Liberal Arts College." *International Journal of Technoethics* 1, pp. 74–91. https://doi.org/10.4018/jte.2010100106

Krause, K., and A.M. Freund. 2014. "How to Beat Procrastination: The Role of Goal Focus." *European Psychologist* 19, pp. 132–144. https://doi.org/10.1027/1016-9040/a000153

Krebs, C.P., C. Lindquist, T. Warner, B. Fisher, and S. Martin. 2007. *The Campus Sexual Assault (CSA) Study: Final Report.* National Criminal Justice Reference Service. http://www.ncjrs.gov/pdffiles1/nij/grants/221153.pdf

Kuh, G.D., T.M. Cruse, R. Shoup, J. Kinzie, and R.M. Gonyea. 2008. "Unmasking the Effects of Student Engagement on First-year College Grades and Persistence." *Journal of Higher Education* 79, pp. 540–563. https://doi.org/10.1353/jhe.0.0019

Kuh, G.D., and S. Hu. 2001. "The Effects of Student-Faculty Interaction in the 1990s." *Review of Higher Education* 24, pp. 309–332. https://doi.org/10.1353/rhe.2001.0005

Lee, C.M., J.L. Maggs, and L.A. Rankin. 2006. "Spring Break Trips as a Risk Factor for Heavy Alcohol Use Among First-year College Students." *Journal of Studies on Alcohol and Drugs* 67, pp. 911–916. https://doi.org/10.15288/jsa.2006.67.911

Lee, R.K. 1998. "Romantic and Electronic Stalking in a College Context." *William & Mary Journal of Women and the Law* 4, pp. 373–466. http://scholarship.law.wm.edu/wmjowl/vol4/iss2/3

Leslie, E., P.B. Sparling, and N. Owen. 2001. "University Campus Settings and the Promotion of Physical Activity in Young Adults: Lessons from Research in Australia and the USA." *Health Education* 10, pp. 116–125. https://doi.org/10.1108/09654280110387880

Levitz, R., and L. Noel. 1989. "Connecting Students to Institutions: Keys to Retention and Success." In *The Freshman Year Experience: Helping Students Survive and Succeed in College,* eds. M.L. Upcraft and J.N. Gardner, pp. 65–81. San Francisco, CA: Jossey-Bass.

Marquis, M. 2005. "Exploring Convenience Orientation as a Food Motivation for College Students Living in Residence Halls." *International Journal of Consumer Studies* 29, pp. 55–63. https://doi.org/10.1111/j.1470-6431.2005.00375.x

Mattanah, J. 2016. *College Student Psychological Adjustment: Exploring Relational Dynamics that Predict Success.* New York, NY: Momentum Press.

Mattanah, J., J. Ayers, B. Brand, L. Brooks, J. Quimby, and S. McNary. 2010. "A Social Support Intervention to Ease the College Transition: Exploring Main Effects and Moderators." *Journal of College Student Development* 51, pp. 93–108. https://doi.org/10.1353/csd.0.0116

Mattanah, J., L. Brooks, B. Brand, J. Quimby, and J. Ayers. 2012. "A Social Support Intervention and Academic Achievement in College: Does Perceived Loneliness Mediate the Relationship?" *Journal of College Counseling* 15, pp. 22–36. https://doi.org/10.1002/j.2161-1882.2012.00003.x

Miles, J.R., and D.M. Kivlighan. 2008. "Team Cognition in Group Interventions: The Relation Between Co-leaders' Shared Mental Models and Group Climate." *Group Dynamics: Theory, Research, and Practice* 12, pp. 191–209. https://doi.org/10.1037/1089-2699.12.3.191

Miles, J.R., and D.M. Kivlighan. 2010. "Co-leader Similarity and Group Climate in Group Interventions: Testing the Co-leadership, Team Cognition-team Diversity Model." *Group Dynamics: Theory, Research, and Practice* 14, pp. 114–122. https://doi.org/10.1037/a0017503

Montmarquette, C., K. Cannings, and S. Mahseredjian. 2002. "How Do Young People Choose College Majors?" *Economics of Education Review* 21, pp. 543–556. https://doi.org/10.1016/s0272-7757(01)00054-1

Nosko, A., and R. Wallace. 1997. "Female/Male Co-leadership in Groups." *Social Work with Groups* 20, pp. 3–16. https://doi.org/10.1300/J009v20n02_02

Olweus, D. 1993. *Bullying at School: What We Know and What We Can Do.* Cambridge: Blackwell.

Olweus, D. 2001. *Olweus' Core Program Against Bullying and Antisocial Behavior: A Teacher Handbook.* Bergen, Norway: HEMIL-Senteret, Universitetet i Bergen.

Oppenheimer, B.T. 1984. "Short-term Small Group Intervention for College Freshmen." *Journal of Counseling Psychology* 31, pp. 45–53. https://doi.org/10.1037/0022-0167.31.1.45

Oswald, D.L., and E.M. Clark. 2003. "Best Friends Forever? High School Best Friendships and the Transition to College." *Personal Relationships* 10, pp. 187–196. https://doi.org/10.1111/1475-6811.00045

Pancer, S.M., B. Hunsberger, M.W. Pratt, and S. Alisat. 2000. "Cognitive Complexity of Expectations and Adjustment to University in the First Year." *Journal of Adolescent Research* 15, pp. 38–57. https://doi.org/10.1177/0743558400151003

Pancer, S.M., M. Pratt, and S. Alisat. 2006. *T2U: A Small Group Intervention to Ease the Transition of First-year Students at University.* Paper Presented at the Biennial Meeting of the Society for Research on Adolescence, San Francisco, California.

Pancer, S.M., M. Pratt, B. Hunsberger, and S. Alisat. 2004. "Bridging Troubled Waters: Helping Students Make the Transition from High School to University."

Guidance and Counselling 19, pp. 184–190. http://www.utpress.utoronto
.ca/GCentre/07784guidco.html

Pascarella, E.T., and P.T. Terenzini. 2005. *How College Affects Students.* San
Francisco, CA: Jossey-Bass.

Paul, E.L., and S. Brier. 2001. "Friendsickness in the Transition to College: Pre-
college Predictors and College Adjustment Correlates." *Journal of Counseling
and Development* 79, pp. 77–89. https://doi.org/10.1002/j.1556-6676.2001.
tb01946.x

Paul, E.L., and K.A. Hayes. 2002. "The Casualties of Casual Sex: A Qualitative Exploration of the Phenomenology of College Students' Hookups."
Journal of Social and Personal Relationships 19, pp. 639–661. https://doi
.org/10.1177/0265407502195006

Paul, E.L., B. McManus, and A. Hayes. 2000. "'Hookups': Characteristics
and Correlates of College Students' Spontaneous and Anonymous Sexual
Experiences." *Journal of Sex Research* 37, pp. 76–88. https://doi.org/10.1080/
00224490009552023

Plant, E.A., K.A. Ericsson, L. Hill, and K. Asberg. 2005. "Why Study Time Does
not Predict Grade Point Average Across College Students: Implications of
Deliberate Practice for Academic Performance." *Contemporary Educational
Psychology* 30, pp. 96–116. https://doi.org/10.1016/j.cedpsych.2004.06.001

Pratt, M.W., B. Hunsberger, S.M. Pancer, S. Alisat, C. Bowers, K. Mackey,
A. Ostaniewicz, E. Rog, B. Terzian, and N. Thomas. 2000. "Facilitating the
Transition to University: Evaluation of a Social Support Discussion Intervention Program." *Journal of College Student Development* 41, pp. 427–441.
https://www.press.jhu.edu/journals/journal-college-student-development

Pritchard, M.E., and G.S. Wilson. 2003. "Using Emotional and Social Factors
to Predict Student Success." *Journal of College Student Development* 44,
pp. 18–28. https://doi.org/10.1353/csd.2003.0008

Radloff, L.S. 1977. "Centre for Epidemiologic Studies Depression Scale." In *Measures of Personality and Social Psychological Attitudes,* eds. J.P. Robinson, P.R.
Shaver, and L.S. Wrightsman, pp. 212–215. Toronto, Canada: Academic Press.

Rickinson, B., and D. Rutherford. 1995. "Increasing Undergraduate Retention
Rates." *British Journal of Guidance & Counseling* 23, pp. 171–172. https://
doi.org/10.1080/03069889508253002

Rose, S. 1984. "How Friendships End: Patterns among Young Adults." *Journal
of Social and Personal Relationships* 1, pp. 267–277. https://doi.org/10.1177/
0265407584013001

Rosenberg, M. 1965. *Society and the Adolescent Self-image.* Princeton, NJ: Princeton
University Press.

Russell, D., L.A. Peplau, and C.E. Cutrona. 1980. "The Revised UCLA Loneliness Scale: Concurrent and Discriminant Validity Evidence." *Journal*

of Personality and Social Psychology 39, pp. 472–480. https://doi.org/
10.1037//0022-3514.39.3.472

Sabella, R.A., J.W. Patchin, and S. Hinduja. 2013. "Cyberbullying Myths and
Realities." *Computers in Human Behavior* 29, pp. 2703–2711. https://doi
.org/10.1016/j.chb.2013.06.040

Sadava, S.W., and A.W. Pak. 1993. "Stress-Related Problem Drinking and
Alcohol Problems: A Longitudinal Study and Extension of Marlatt's Model."
Canadian Journal of Behavioural Science 25, pp. 446–464. https://doi
.org/10.1037/h0078841

Schenk, A.M., and W.J. Fremouw. 2012. "Prevalence, Psychological Impact, and
Coping of Cyberbully Victims among College Students." *Journal of School
Violence* 11, pp. 21–37. https://doi.org/10.1080/15388220.2011.630310

Schenk, A.M., W.J. Fremouw, and C.M. Keelan. 2013. "Characteristics of
College Cyberbullies." *Computers in Human Behavior* 29, pp. 2320–2327.
https://doi.org/10.1016/j.chb.2013.05.013

Schwarzer, R., and M. Jerusalem. 1995. "Generalized Self-efficacy Scale." In
Measures in Health Psychology: A User's Portfolio, Causal and Control Beliefs,
eds. J. Weinman, S. Wright, and M. Johnston, pp. 35–37. Windsor, UK:
Nfer-nelson.

Scopelliti, M., and L. Tiberio. 2010. "Homesickness in University Students:
The Role of Multiple Place Attachment." *Environment and Behavior* 42,
pp. 335–350. https://doi.org/10.1177/0013916510361872

Shim, S., and A. Ryan. 2012. "What Do Students Want Socially When they Arrive
at College? Implications of Social Achievement Goals for Social Behaviors and
Adjustment during the First Semester of College." *Motivation and Emotion* 36,
pp. 1–12. https://doi.org/10.1007/s11031-011-9272-3

Tao, S., Q. Dong, M.W. Pratt, B. Hunsberger, and S.M. Pancer. 2000. "Social
Support: Relations to Coping and Adjustment during the Transition to
University in the People's Republic of China." *Journal of Adolescent Research*
15, pp. 123–144. https://doi.org/10.1177/0743558400151007

Thorson, A. 2005. "The Effect of College Major on Wages." *Park Place Economist*
13, pp. 45–57. https://www-test.iwu.edu/economics/PPE13/thorson.pdf

Thurber C.A., and E.A. Walton. 2012. "Homesickness and Adjustment in
University Students." *Journal of American College Health* 60, pp. 415–419.
https://doi.org/10.1080/07448481.2012.673520

Tice, D., and R.F. Baumeister. 1997. "Longitudinal Study of Procrastination, Performance, Stress, and Health: The Cost and Benefits of Dawdling." *Psychological
Science* 8, pp. 454–458. https://doi.org/10.1111/j.1467-9280.1997.tb00460.x

Tomsich, E.A., L.M. Schiable, C.M. Rennison, and A.R. Gover. 2013. "Violent
Victimization and Hooking Up among Strangers and Acquaintances on an
Urban Campus: An Exploratory Study." *Criminal Justice Studies: A Critical*

Journal of Crime, Law, and Society 26, pp. 433–454. https://doi.org/10.1080/1478601X.2013.842564

Trockel, M.T., M.D. Barnes, and D.L. Egget. 2000. "Health-related Variables and Academic Performance among First-year College Students: Implications for Sleep and Other Behaviors." *Journal of American College Health* 49, pp. 125–131. https://doi.org/10.1080/07448480009596294

Tuckman, B.W., and M.A.C. Jensen. 1977. "Stages of Small-Group Development Revisited." *Group & Organization Management* 2, pp. 419–427. https://doi.org/105960117700200404

Upcraft, M.L., J.N. Gardner, and B.O. Barefoot. 2005. *Challenging and Supporting the First-year Student: A Handbook for Improving the First Year of College.* San Francisco, CA: Jossey-Bass.

Walker, J.K., N.D. Martin, and A. Hussey. 2015. "Greek Organization Membership and Collegiate Outcomes at an Elite, Private University." *Research in Higher Education* 56, pp. 203–227. https://doi.org/10.1007/s11162-014-9345-8

Wechsler, H., J.E. Lee, M. Kuo, M. Seibring, T.F. Nelson, and H. Lee. 2002. "Trends in College Binge Drinking During a Period of Increased Prevention Efforts: Findings from Four Harvard School of Public Health College Alcohol Study Surveys: 1993–2001." *Journal of American College Health* 50, pp. 203–217. https://doi.org/10.1080/07448480209595713

Wensley, K., and M. Campbell. 2012. "Heterosexual and Non-heterosexual Young University Students' Involvement in Traditional and Cyber Forms of Bullying." *Cyberpsychology, Behavior, and Social Networking* 15, pp. 649–654. https://doi.org/10.1089/cyber.2012.0132

Wilcox, P., S. Winn, and M. Fyvie-Gauld. 2005. "It Was Nothing to Do with the University, It Was the People: The Role of Social Support in the First-year Experience of Higher Education." *Studies in Higher Education* 30, pp. 707–722. https://doi.org/10.1080/03075070500340036

Wintre, M.G., S.K.E. Gates, S.M. Pancer, M.W. Pratt, J. Polivy, S. Birnie-Lefcovitch, and G. Adams. 2009. "The Student Perception of University Support & Structure Scale: Development and Validation." *Journal of Youth Studies* 12, pp. 289–306. https://doi.org/10.1080/13676260902775085

Wintre, M.G., G.M. Knoll, S.M. Pancer, M.W. Pratt, J. Polivy, S. Birnie-Lefcovitch, and G.R. Adams. 2008. "The Transition to University: The Student-University Match (SUM) Questionnaire." *Journal of Adolescent Research* 23, pp. 745–769. https://doi.org/10.1177/0743558408325972

Wolf, T.M., P.L. Scurria, and M.G. Webster. 1998. "A Four-year Study of Anxiety, Depression, Loneliness, Social Support, and Perceived Mistreatment in Medical Students." *Journal of Health Psychology* 3, pp. 125–136. https://doi.org/10.1177/135910539800300110

About the Author

Melinda S. Harper, PhD, is professor of psychology at Queens University of Charlotte. She introduced and continues to co-direct the Transition to University (T2U) program. She and her co-author, Dr. Christine Allegretti, have published a number of articles and presented empirical research about the T2U program. In addition to her teaching and research, Dr. Harper also maintains an active clinical practice as a psychologist and partner of Charlotte Psychotherapy & Consultation Group. Her primary clinical focus is on assisting adolescents and young adults with normative transitions in their lives, including the transition from high school to college and from college to the workforce.

Christine L. Allegretti, PhD, is professor of psychology at Queens University of Charlotte. Along with Dr. Melinda Harper, she introduced and continues to co-direct the Transition to University (T2U) program. Her research interests are in the areas of critical thinking, loneliness, and first-year student adjustment. In addition to teaching in the Department of Psychology, she has taught in the first-year core curriculum program, organized a first-year experience program, and served as chair of psychology and chair of social sciences at Queens. She was also the recipient of the William S. Lee Teaching Award at Queens University of Charlotte.

Index

OTHER TITLES IN OUR PSYCHOLOGY COLLECTION

Announcing Digital Content Crafted by Librarians

CPSIA information can be obtained
at www.ICGtesting.com
Printed in the USA
JSHW021335250819
1166JS00006B/10

9 781946 646088